Patterson's

Standing Strong

Daily Devotional and Study Guide

Volume 1

Patterson's
Standing Strong

Daily Devotional and Study Guide

Includes
Scriptures, Interpretations,
Definitions, Prayers, Inspirational Messages,
and Activities

Volume 1

By

David Patterson

Patterson's Standing Strong, Daily Devotional and Study Guide, Volume 1

Copyright © 2022 by David Patterson

ISBN: 979-8-9873164-1-2

Name: Patterson, David, author.
Title: Patterson's Standing Strong, Daily Devotional and Study Guide, Volume 1

Patterson's Standing Strong, Daily Devotional and Study Guide, Volume 1 ISBN 979-8-9873164-1-2

King James Version (KJV) Public Domain

Cover Design by David Patterson

Dedicated to my…

Lord and Savior Jesus the Christ

Family

Brothers and Sisters in Christ

Regardless of how the world sees me or what the world tries to tell me about myself, my faith, or my life... I know that I am perfect because God said that I am perfect. Only my God knows what to change in me and when to change it, not this world. What this world finds important, is not important to my God. Therefore, I will continue to listen, follow and put all my trust in my God.

~David Patterson

Table of Contents

My Confession to Become Saved

How can I be saved?

Going from being a sinner to being saved is easy and only requires believing and having faith. Making this decision will take you from being hell-bound to being heaven-bound, from the law to grace, and from death to eternal life.

So what does it really mean to believe and to have faith?

Well, before we can begin to answer that question, we must first understand the ideas of "belief" and "faith" in a way that we can both visualize and relate to. This can be accomplished by using something as simple as a chair to give you something you can visualize and relate to.

Now consider this example:

You are exhausted and feeling faint, and desperately need to sit down. You look all around the room and can only find a wobbly old wooden chair where parts of the back are missing, the seat is broken up, and the overall appearance is not too reassuring. Nevertheless, you need to sit down and rest before something bad happens. so you rush over to the chair, sit down, and rest. You sit there until the faint feeling passes, and after you are rested, you arise from the chair.

What was seen in this example was both "belief' and "faith." You may ask yourself, "How does sitting in a chair show belief and faith?" Well, you used belief when you believed that the chair would be able to support your body weight; even if you pushed on the seat before sitting down, there was no guarantee that it would support your full body weight. And as soon as you sat down, you used faith.

You see, to believe in something means that you have trust in it, regardless of how things may seem, feel, sound, or even look. Faith becomes available only after belief is present, because it acts on what was believed. In other words, belief is vision, and faith is action. And those two things are the only requirements to be saved.

But can it be that easy?

Yes! Going from being a sinner to being saved is as easy as sitting in a chair.

What does it mean to be a Christian?

In order to understand what it means to be a Christian, we first have to find out what the word actually means. Christian comes from the Greek word Christianos, which comes from the word Christos. Christianos simply means "followers of Christ," and Christos simply means "anointed." Going from Christos to Christianos is similar to the concept of going from the word "America" to "American." That change is important because it means that you belong to something, which in this example is America.

Jesus was called by many names, and one of those most prominent names was "The Christ." At times both names were combined and he was called "Jesus Christ." So by saying that you are a Christian, you are saying that you have accepted and belong to Jesus. In other words, you follow Jesus the Christ. Regardless of what religious title you align with or by which one of Jesus' many names you call him, accepting Jesus as your Lord and Savior makes you a Christian.

Accepting Jesus

When you accept Jesus, you become one of his disciples and represent his grace, mercy, and love. In this world, Jesus' ways and teachings are commonly misinterpreted, abused, and used to manipulate others to spread hate, push personal biases and opinions, or for other self-serving reasons. Therefore, it is important to learn Jesus' ways and understand his teachings for yourself, which requires reading the Word and doing the research. It is not important to argue titles or which style of worship to Christ is correct, for they all are meant to give genuine praises to Christ and the Father.

Do not be confused: Since Jesus fulfilled the law, the only way to heaven, everlasting life, and the Father is through Jesus. There were many great prophets, philosophers, teachers, preachers, martyrs, leaders, and wise men who had great messages that can positively impact your life, but there is only one way to heaven, and that is through Jesus the Christ.

Accepting Jesus as your Lord and Savior is quick and easy. All that is required is that you believe and have faith. By saying the Last Confession as a Sinner in the next section, you are showing that you believe and have faith. Just forming the words to speak out of your mouth to accept Jesus as your Lord and Savior shows belief, just like making the effort to sit in that old wobbly wooden chair we discussed earlier. Faith is the action shown by completing the confession, just like the action of sitting in that same chair from earlier.

Jesus loves you so much that he made becoming saved simple. So simple that all you have to do is make a confession to him of your belief in him. Whether or not you feel anything during or after this confession does not change the fact that you became saved. After this confession, you are no longer a sinner, because you have accepted the finished works of Jesus, one of which is the remission of sin. That is why I call it the Last Confession as a Sinner, because anything you confess or do going forward will be done as a Christian and not as a sinner. The devil's job is to attack your belief and faith by trying to convince you that you are not saved and that you are still a sinner. Do not let him win. Stand strong on your belief and stand strong on your faith to know that Jesus loves you and you are saved.

The Last Confession as a Sinner

This is the last confession you make as a sinner, because once you are finished, you will no longer be a sinner. This confession is between you and Jesus, with God bearing witness.

Are you ready to be set free? If so, let's begin:

Jesus the Christ, the son of the living God, I confess with my mouth that I accept you as the Lord of my life and as my savior. I believe that you were perfect in every way, fulfilling the law and became the perfect sacrifice to die for all of my sins so that I can live. I believe that God raised you from the dead, and that you rose with all power in your hands. I believe that you sat down your glory to come to earth, in order to make it easy for me to be saved and heaven bound.

I believe that you are the son of God, and that no one can come to the Father unless it is by you alone. I believe that you are the way, the truth, and the life. I believe that you are alive and seated at the right hand of God in the heavens above and I believe that you will watch over me because you love me. And now I can say that I love you, because you first loved me. Thank you, my Lord. Thank you, my God.

This is my confession, and right now I receive your spirit, Lord Jesus, and right now, I am saved, no longer a sinner, and heaven-bound. I am free from guilt and shame. I no longer have to worry about what I did before this confession, because I am now saved and Jesus' sacrifice, love, and mercy just took care of it all. Jesus forgave me, and now I forgive myself and let it go.

I am a new creation, forever in your love, mercy, and grace, Lord Jesus. I give my life to you, my Lord, and I will follow your commandment to love each other for the rest of my days.

A new work has begun in me, and I will focus on what you tell me, my Lord, and no longer focus on what the world tells me. I answer only to you, my Lord, and no longer answer to the world. Thank you for freeing me, Jesus. I love you. Amen.

Congratulations, and welcome to the family. You will never have to say that confession again to be saved because only God can reverse it, and no matter what you do, he never will, because he loves you too much. So remove all doubt, because this is a done deal. Live your life for God, live your life for Jesus, and live your life in love.

God bless you.

Introduction

Congratulations! You have in your hands a great tool that will help you on your journey towards understanding the Bible. I am starting this introduction with a couple of examples from typical scenarios that you have probably either experienced or can relate to: receiving a gift from a loved one; and having your hard work undone. These examples will help get you in the right mindset in order to understand the Word. This mindset or understanding you will get from these examples is not limited to this study guide, but should be applied throughout your journey.

Example 1: You just received a gift from a loved one and responded to them by saying, "This is real nice."

Knowing that this scenario involves receiving a gift from a loved one, we can begin to examine it. When we look up the word "nice" in the dictionary, we find that it is defined using the words "pleasant," "agreeable," and "satisfactory." Based on your response, "This is real nice," we can draw the conclusion that you not only appreciated the gift, but also enjoyed it.

Example 2: You ran an errand after cleaning your place and return to find it a mess. Once you see this, you say, "This is real nice," to your loved ones.

Knowing that this scenario involves disappointment and frustration, we can begin to examine it. Once again, if we turn to the dictionary, we can draw the conclusion that you enjoyed or approved your loved ones actions.

Although the phrase "this is real nice" was used in both examples, by considering the context we know their meaning is not the same. However, if the context is not considered, the second example would have been misinterpreted or wrongly divided and lead someone to believe that you enjoyed having your place messed up. This is also true with the Word of God and is why understanding the definition of a word is important, but understanding its context is critical.

In this devotional and study guide, you will not only be given the scriptures but also definitions along with a definition based on the context. Some of the words and expressions used in the Bible are no longer used; therefore, this guide will include a modern word or expression that you can substitute to help with your understanding. In some cases, just understanding what the word or expression means will give you an accurate and deeper understanding.

This guide will walk you through a number of scriptures that are grouped together under a common topic that will impact your everyday life. There's not a time limit or a certain number of verses or chapters to finish each day, because everyone is different. What is important is being present and consistent with this guide. Do not feel that you have to understand every scripture the first time you read it; this is impossible. The goal is to understand as much as you can, and then move on. You can come back later after exploring other scriptures in this guide. As you surround yourself with the Word daily, you will continue to crave a deeper understanding, and the Lord will start to reveal more and more of himself to you and increase your understanding. You can review this book in its entirety several times to keep getting a deeper understanding.

Being present and consistent is the key to true understanding, because the Lord will show you what his Word means, little by little, even things lost in translation. Prepare your mind by praying to the Lord before you start studying. Pray that the Lord unlocks his Word to you and remember that God is love. If you find anything that does not line up with God's love, mercy, or grace, it is a good indicator that you may not be rightly dividing the Word or need to expand the number of verses and/or chapters you must read to understand the context.

Remember: Understanding the Bible is a life-long journey, so let's begin!

Chapter 1

I Believe In Jesus; I Believe In God

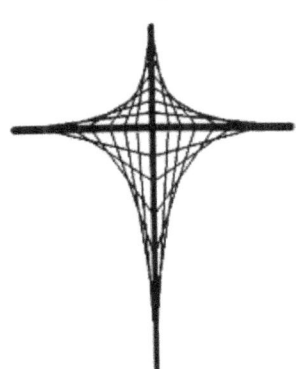

*F*or everything in our lives is temporary. This applies to both the good and especially the bad; the positive and the negative. This could be overwhelming and depressing to think about because we do not want to think of all the good and positive things in our lives as being only temporary. In such a negative world, we do not want to lose the little bit of good we have left. But in the reality of a believer, we know the Lord's blessings are endless and we receive blessing after blessing. As followers of Christ, we have this wonderful benefit and advantage over non-believers because anything good or positive in our lives never runs out because it comes from the Lord.

*I*n order to understand the benefit and need for all good and positive things to be temporary, I want you to imagine that you are watching your favorite movie or listening to your favorite song or performing one of your favorite pastime activities... now imagine if you could only do this one thing all the time. Would it still bring you the same joy? Would it still make you happy? What if you were still doing the same thing after a few hours, days, weeks, months, or years had passed? I imagine that it would no longer bring you the same joy it once did. Why? Because what makes these things so special is that you get to experience them in that moment.

So whatever you may be going through right now, just know that it will get better. Because whatever problems you are going through, they are only temporary and they will pass. And once they have passed, they will be replaced by wonderful gifts from the Father. If you are not going through anything right now, take the time to enjoy the things around you and know that when that fades away or dies, what will come next will be even better.

How do you know that the next thing will be better? Because you serve a merciful God and every good and perfect gift comes from Him. God will never "bless" you, a believer, with something bad or negative. So, if you are in Christ, then this applies to you and you have a God-given right to expect and receive God's blessings in your life. Your blessing awaits... receive it now in Jesus' name.

Scripture 1
Romans 8:18-30 KJV

18 For I reckon that the sufferings of this present time are not worthy to be compared with the glory which shall be revealed in us.

19 For the earnest expectation of the creature waiteth for the manifestation of the sons of God.

20 For the creature was made subject to vanity, not willingly, but by reason of him who hath subjected the same in hope,

21 Because the creature itself also shall be delivered from the bondage of corruption into the glorious liberty of the children of God.

22 For we know that the whole creation groaneth and travaileth in pain together until now.

23 And not only they, but ourselves also, which have the firstfruits of the Spirit, even we ourselves groan within ourselves, waiting for the adoption, to wit, the redemption of our body.

24 For we are saved by hope: but hope that is seen is not hope: for what a man seeth, why doth he yet hope for?

25 But if we hope for that we see not, then do we with patience wait for it.

26 Likewise the Spirit also helpeth our infirmities: for we know not what we should pray for as we ought: but the Spirit itself maketh intercession for us with groanings which cannot be uttered.

27 And he that searcheth the hearts knoweth what is the mind of the Spirit, because he maketh intercession for the saints according to the will of God.

28 And we know that all things work together for good to them that love God, to them who are the called according to his purpose.

29 For whom he did foreknow, he also did predestinate to be conformed to the image of his Son, that he might be the firstborn among many brethren.

30 Moreover whom he did predestinate, them he also called: and whom he called, them he also justified: and whom he justified, them he also glorified.

Romans 8:18-30 Clarification

[18] We should not focus on the pain and struggles we currently face by being a believer because it does not compare to all the glory that is already inside of us. This glory will be revealed in the believer.

[19-21] For all things created by God eagerly wait for the Children of God to be revealed. The things God created are frustrated with waiting because their waiting is not due to their own doing, but because God subjected them to wait. Once the Children of God is revealed, all Creation will be set free from the bondage of decay and brought into freedom and glory of the children of God.

[22] We know that the things God created have been groaning and in agony until now.

[23] And not only them, but us, who have the best of the spirit, we quietly suffer as well, while we wait for our bodies to become aware and accepted to the family by the father.

[24] We were saved by belief. But belief in what you can see does not require belief at all. Who believes for something that they already have or see?

[25] But if we believe for something that we do not have or see, we wait for it patiently.

[26] In the same way, the Spirit helps us in our weakness. We do not know what we should pray for, but the Spirit itself speaks for us through a sacred language.

[27] And he who looks into our hearts knows the mind of the Spirit, because the Spirit speaks for God's people in accordance with the will of God.

[28] And we know that all things will work out for the good of those who love God, of whom are called according to his purpose.

29 For those who God knew before conception, he aligned their fate so they reflect the image of his Son, so he can be the firstborn among many brothers and sisters.

30 Of them that were fated, he also called; of them that were called, he also made righteous; Of them that were made righteous, he made excellent.

Definitions

Creature
Word Definition:
Something made: animal or human
Contextual Definition:
All things that were created by God
Substitution Word/phrase for clarity:
"all things created by God"

Sons of God
Word Definition:
N/A
Contextual Definition:
The sons and daughters of God who believe in God and Jesus. If they were alive before Jesus' birth, it is the ones who accepted God as their father. If they were alive after Jesus' birth, it is the ones who accepted God as their father and Jesus as their Lord and savior.
Substitution Word/phrase for clarity:
"Sons of God"

Travaileth
Word Definition:
Painful or difficult work; Labor pains
Contextual Definition:
Constantly suffering in pain similar to a woman suffering during the birth of a child
Substitution Word/phrase for clarity:
"agony"

Firstfruits
Word Definition:
The initial or first of something produced or gathered
Contextual Definition:
The most special among similar things
Substitution Word/phrase for clarity:
"best"

Groan within ourselves
Word Definition:
N/A
Contextual Definition:
To be upset or disheartened but not say anything or physically express it
Substitution Word/phrase for clarity:
"Quietly suffers"

Wit
Word Definition:
To know; have awareness; have the ability to learn
Contextual Definition:
To become aware
Substitution Word/phrase for clarity:
"aware"

Intercession
Word Definition:
To take an action on someone's behalf
Contextual Definition:
To speak on behalf of someone else

Substitution Word/phrase for clarity:
"speaks"

Groanings which cannot be uttered
Word Definition:
N/A
Contextual Definition:
To make sounds like speaking but without using your native language
Substitution Word/phrase for clarity:
"a sacred language"

Foreknow
Word Definition:
Be aware or know something ahead of time
Contextual Definition:
To know someone before they came into existence
Substitution Word/phrase for clarity:
"knew before conception"

Predestine
Word Definition:
Determined ahead of time by higher power; fate
Contextual Definition:
Preplanned
Substitution Word/phrase for clarity:
"fated"

Conformed
Word Definition:
To act in accordance to an acceptable standard, person or idea
Contextual Definition:
To behave like someone else
Substitution Word/phrase for clarity:
"reflect"

Justified
Word Definition:
To be made or appointed righteous in God's eyes. To do something good or just
Contextual Definition:
To make someone righteous
Substitution Word/phrase for clarity:
"made righteous"

Glorified
Word Definition:
To give praise; to elevate or to worship someone or something.
Contextual Definition:
To be treated as being more excellent. Distinguished among all others.
Substitution Word/phrase for clarity:
"made excellent" or "made special"

Scripture 2
Isaiah 53 KJV

1 Who hath believed our report? and to whom is the arm of the Lord revealed?

2 For he shall grow up before him as a tender plant, and as a root out of a dry ground: he hath no form nor comeliness; and when we shall see him, there is no beauty that we should desire him.

3 He is despised and rejected of men; a man of sorrows, and acquainted with grief: and we hid as it were our faces from him; he was despised, and we esteemed him not.

4 Surely he hath borne our griefs, and carried our sorrows: yet we did esteem him stricken, smitten of God, and afflicted.

5 But he was wounded for our transgressions, he was bruised for our iniquities: the chastisement of our peace was upon him; and with his stripes we are healed.

6 All we like sheep have gone astray; we have turned every one to his own way; and the Lord hath laid on him the iniquity of us all.

7 He was oppressed, and he was afflicted, yet he opened not his mouth: he is brought as a lamb to the slaughter, and as a sheep before her shearers is dumb, so he openeth not his mouth.

8 He was taken from prison and from judgment: and who shall declare his generation? for he was cut off out of the land of the living: for the transgression of my people was he stricken.

9 And he made his grave with the wicked, and with the rich in his death; because he had done no violence, neither was any deceit in his mouth.

10 Yet it pleased the Lord to bruise him; he hath put him to grief: when thou shalt make his soul an offering for sin, he shall see his seed, he shall prolong his days, and the pleasure of the Lord shall prosper in his hand.

11 He shall see of the travail of his soul, and shall be satisfied: by his knowledge shall my righteous servant justify many; for he shall bear their iniquities.

12 Therefore will I divide him a portion with the great, and he shall

divide the spoil with the strong; because he hath poured out his soul unto death: and he was numbered with the <u>transgressors</u>; and he bare the sin of many, and made intercession for the transgressors.

Isaiah 53 Clarification

1 Who believed our report? Who has the Lord revealed his strength to?

2 Jesus grew up before God like a gentle plant, but out of place like a root coming out of dry ground. Jesus did not have a desirable appearance; and when we saw him, there was no beauty that we should lust after him.

3 Jesus was despised and rejected by men; Jesus was a man of sorrows, and acquainted with grief, and we hid our faces from him. Jesus was despised and we did not desire to be him.

4 Surely Jesus carried our griefs and carried our sorrows: we acknowledge that he was stricken, physically punished by God, and afflicted.

5 But Jesus was wounded for our transgressions, he was bruised for our sinful behavior. The punishment for our peace was placed on him and with his stripes we are healed.

6 Just like sheep, we have all gone astray. Everyone turning to their own ways; but the Lord laid on him all of our sinful behaviors.

7 Jesus was oppressed, and was afflicted, but he did not open his mouth because he was brought like a lamb to the slaughter. And as a sheep before the shearers' remains silent, so did Jesus.

8 Jesus was taken from prison and judgment. But who from his generation spoke up? For he was cut off from the land of the living because of the sins of my generation. That is why he was stricken.

9 Jesus made his grave with the wicked and the rich in his death but he was not violent, neither did he speak anything deceitful.

10 Yet it pleased the Lord to bruise Jesus; he had to place mankind's grief on Jesus because the Lord had to make his soul an offering for sin. The Lord sees his seed, and will

prolong his days and the pleasure of the Lord shall prosper in his hands. [11] The Lord shall see the trail of Jesus' soul, and will be satisfied. Because of the Lord's knowledge, he knows that his righteous servant will justify many and he will bear their sinful behaviors. [12] Therefore I will divide him a portion with the great, and he shall divide the spoil with the strong; because he poured out his soul unto his death and he was numbered with the sinners; and he bares the sin of many, and made intercession for the sinners.

Definitions

Comeliness
> Word Definition:
>> Pleasing in appearance; attractive
>
> Contextual Definition:
>> Something desirable or enticing
>
> Substitution Word/phrase for clarity:
>> "desirable appearance"

Esteemed
> Word Definition:
>> To be respected or highly valued
>
> Contextual Definition:
>> To envy or want to be someone
>
> Substitution Word/phrase for clarity:
>> "desired to be"

Borne
> Word Definition:
>> To be transported or carried by something
>
> Contextual Definition:
>> To take something on that's not yours
>
> Substitution Word/phrase for clarity:
>> "carried"

Smitten
> Word Definition:
>> To strike someone or something hard with the hand

> Contextual Definition:
>> To punish by force for wrongdoing
>
> Substitution Word/phrase for clarity:
>> "physically punished by"

Iniquities
> Word Definition:
>> Immoral behavior or actions; wickedness; an extreme injustice
>
> Contextual Definition:
>> Behavior not pleasing to God
>
> Substitution Word/phrase for clarity:
>> "sinful behavior"

Chastisement
> Word Definition:
>> To punish or whip someone; To censure or rebuke
>
> Contextual Definition:
>> To punish
>
> Substitution Word/phrase for clarity:
>> "punishment for"

Shearers
> Word Definition:
>> To cut or remove something
>
> Contextual Definition:
>> To remove hair
>
> Substitution Word/phrase for clarity:
>> "Shearer"

Travail

Word Definition:
  Painful or difficult work;
  Labor pains
Contextual Definition:
  A painful trial
Substitution Word/phrase for clarity:
  "trial"

Transgressors

Word Definition:
  To sin or violate a rule, law, or command
Contextual Definition:
  A sinner
Substitution Word/phrase for clarity:
  "sinners"

Psalms 31 KJV

¹ In You, O LORD, I put my trust; Let me never be ashamed; Deliver me in Your righteousness.

² Bow down Your ear to me, Deliver me peedily; Be my rock of refuge, A fortress of defense to save me.

³ For You are my rock and my fortress; Therefore, for Your name's sake, Lead me and guide me.

⁴ Pull me out of the net which they have secretly laid for me, For You are my strength.

⁵ Into Your hand I commit my spirit; You have redeemed me, O LORD God of truth.

⁶ I have hated those who regard useless idols;
But I trust in the LORD.

⁷ I will be glad and rejoice in Your mercy, For You have considered my trouble; You have known my soul in adversities, ⁸ And have not shut me up into the hand of the enemy;
You have set my feet in a wide place.

⁹ Have mercy on me, O LORD, for I am in trouble;
My eye wastes away with grief,
Yes, my soul and my body!

¹⁰ For my life is spent with grief.
And my years with sighing;
My strength fails because of my iniquity,
And my bones waste away.

¹¹ I am a reproach among all my enemies,
But especially among my neighbors,
And am repulsive to my acquaintances;
Those who see me outside flee from me.

¹² I am forgotten like a dead man, out of mind;
I am like a broken vessel.

¹³ For I hear the slander of many;
Fear is on every side; While they take counsel together against me, They scheme to take away my life.

¹⁴ But as for me, I trust in You, O LORD;
I say. "You are my God."

¹⁵ My times are in Your hand; Deliver me from the hand of my enemies,
And from those who persecute me.

¹⁶ Make Your face shine upon Your servant;
Save me for Your mercies' sake.
¹⁷ Do not let me be ashamed, O LORD, for I have called upon You; Let the wicked be ashamed;
Let them be silent in the grave.
¹⁸ Let the lying lips be put to silence, Which speak insolent things proudly and contemptuously against the righteous.
¹⁹ Oh, how great is Your goodness, Which You have laid up for those who fear You, Which You have prepared for those who trust in You In the presence of the sons of men!
²⁰ You shall hide them in the secret place of Your presence From the plots of man;

You shall keep them secretly in a pavilion
From the strife of tongues.
²¹ Blessed be the LORD, For He has shown me His marvelous kindness in a strong city!
²² For I said in my haste, "I am cut off from before Your eyes";
Nevertheless You heard the voice of my supplications When I cried out to You.
²³ Oh, love the LORD, all you His saints! For the LORD preserves the faithful, And fully repays the proud person.
²⁴ Be of good courage, And He shall strengthen your heart, All you who hope in the LORD.

Psalms 31 Clarification

¹ My Lord, I put my trust in you; Do not let me be ashamed. Deliver me with your righteousness.
² Please listen to me, and quickly deliver me; Be my rock of refuge, my protection to save me.
³ For You are my rock and my fortress; Therefore, for Your name's sake, Lead me and guide me.

⁴ Pull me out of the net which they have secretly laid for me, For You are my strength.
⁵ Into Your hand I commit my spirit; You have saved me, O Lord God of truth.
⁶ I have hated those who regard useless idols; But I trust in the Lord.
⁷ I will be glad and rejoice in your mercy that you have shown me in

listening to my trouble. You know how my soul is when it's in trouble. ⁸ And have not turned me over to my enemy; you have set my feet on stable land.

⁹ Oh Lord, have mercy on me because I am in trouble. Grief has brought me to constant tears, so much that it has affected both my soul and my body. ¹⁰ My life is filled with grief, and my years with sighing; my sin has taken my strength, and my body wasted away.

¹¹ I am a disappointment to all my enemies, but especially to people around me. Repulsive to my acquaintances. Those who see me outside, run away from me.

¹² I am treated like I don't exist and out of my mind. I am like a broken vessel.

¹³ For I hear the slander from many people; Fear is on every side. They gather to plot against me. They scheme ways to try and kill me.

¹⁴ Despite where I am, I trust you Lord. I say "You are my God."

¹⁵ My life is in your hands; Deliver me from the hands of my enemies, and those who plot against me.

¹⁶ Make Your face shine upon Your servant; Save me for Your mercies' sake.

¹⁷ Do not let me be ashamed, O Lord, for I have called upon You; Let the wicked be ashamed; Let them be silent in the grave.

¹⁸ Silence the lying lips, which speak disrespectable things proudly and show disrespect against the righteous.

¹⁹ Oh, how great is Your goodness, Which You prepared for those who fear You and those who trust in You, In the presence of everyone!

²⁰ You shall hide them from any schemes in your presence; You shall keep them secretly in a Shelter from the strife of tongues.

²¹ Blessed be the Lord, For He has shown me His marvelous kindness in a strong city!

²² For I mistakenly said that you no longer see me. Despite that, you still heard my requests when I cried out to you.

²³ Oh, love the Lord, all you His saints! For the Lord preserves the faithful, And fully repays the proud person.

[24] Be of good courage, And He shall strengthen your heart, All you who hope in the Lord.

Definitions

Peedily
Word Definition:
N/A
Contextual Definition:
Something that happens quickly or very fast
Substitution Word/phrase for clarity:
"quickly"

Redeemed
Word Definition:
To be restored from any faults or consequences by a form of payment; Cleared
Contextual Definition:
To be saved from wrongdoing
Substitution Word/phrase for clarity:
"saved"

Adversities
Word Definition:
Ongoing difficulty or misfortune
Contextual Definition:
Trouble
Substitution Word/phrase for clarity:
"Trouble"

Reproach
Word Definition:
Disapproval or disappointment; Blame
Contextual Definition:
Disapproval or disappointment; Blame

Substitution Word/phrase for clarity:
"disappointment"

Persecute
Word Definition:
To show hostility towards someone as a form of punishment because of something disliked
Contextual Definition:
To deliberately show hostility towards someone for public humiliation
Substitution Word/phrase for clarity:
"plot against"

Insolent
Word Definition:
Being rude, arrogant and disrespectful
Contextual Definition:
To verbally disrespect someone
Substitution Word/phrase for clarity:
"disrespectable"

Contemptuously
Word Definition:
To show or feel extreme hatred to someone
Contextual Definition:
Showing disrespect towards someone
Substitution Word/phrase for clarity:
"show disrespect"

Sons of men
Word Definition:
N/A
Contextual Definition:
all mankind
Substitution Word/phrase for clarity:
"everyone"

Pavilion
Word Definition:
A decorative building, structure or tent
Contextual Definition:
A shelter or fort
Substitution Word/phrase for clarity:
"Shelter"

Supplications
Word Definition:
To genuinely ask or beg for something in a humbling or sincere way
Contextual Definition:
Repeated requests or begging
Substitution Word/phrase for clarity:
"Requests"

Scripture 4
Deuteronomy 1:19-33 KJV

19 And when we departed from Horeb, we went through all that great and terrible <u>wilderness</u>, which ye saw by the way of the mountain of the Amorites, as the LORD our God commanded us; and we came to Kadeshbarnea.

20 And I said unto you, Ye are come unto the mountain of the Amorites, which the LORD our God doth give unto us.

21 Behold, the LORD thy God hath set the land before thee: go up and <u>possess</u> it, as the LORD God of thy fathers hath said unto thee; fear not, neither be discouraged.

22 And ye came near unto me every one of you, and said, We will send men before us, and they shall search us out the land, and bring us word again by what way we must go up, and into what cities we shall come.

23 And the saying pleased me well: and I took twelve men of you, one of a tribe: 24 And they turned and went up into the mountain, and came unto the valley of Eshcol, and searched it out.

25 And they took of the fruit of the land in their hands, and brought it down unto us, and brought us word again, and said, It is a good land which the LORD our God doth give us.

26 Notwithstanding ye would not go up, but rebelled against the commandment of the LORD your God:

27 And ye murmured in your tents, and said, Because the LORD hated us, he hath brought us forth out of the land of Egypt, to deliver us into the hand of the Amorites, to destroy us.

28 Whither shall we go up? our brethren have discouraged our heart, saying, The people is greater and taller than we; the cities are great and walled up to heaven, and moreover we have seen the sons of the Anakims there.

29 Then I said unto you, Dread not, neither be afraid of them.

30 The LORD your God which goeth before you, he shall fight for you, according to all that he did for you in Egypt before your eyes; 31 And in the wilderness, where thou hast seen how that the LORD thy God bare

thee, as a man doth bear his son, in all the way that ye went, until ye came into this place. ³² Yet in this thing ye did not believe the Lᴏʀᴅ your God, ³³ Who went in the way before you, to search you out a place to pitch your tents in, in fire by night, to shew you by what way ye should go, and in a cloud by day.

Deuteronomy 1:19-33 Clarification

¹⁹ "When we departed from Horeb, and went through all that great and terrible desert which you saw on the way to the mountains of the Amorites, as the Lord our God had commanded us. Then we came to Kadesh Barnea.

²⁰ And I said to you, 'You have come to the mountains of the Amorites, which the Lord our God has given to us.

²¹ Behold, the Lord your God has set the land before you; go up and take it, as the Lord God of your fathers has spoken to you; do not fear or be discouraged.'

²² "And every one of you came near to me and said, 'We will send men ahead of us, and let them scope out the land for us, and tell us how we should proceed, and the cities we will see.'

²³ "I liked the plan; so I took twelve of your men, one man from each tribe.

²⁴ And they departed and went up into the mountains, and came to the Valley of Eshcol, and scoped it out.

²⁵ They also took some of the fruit of the land in their hands and brought it down to us; and they brought back word to us, saying, 'It is a good land which the Lord our God is giving us.'

²⁶ "However, you would not go up, but rebelled against the commandment of the Lord your God; ²⁷ and you complained in your tents, and said, 'Because the Lord hates us, He has brought us from the land of Egypt just to deliver us into the hand of the Amorites, to destroy us.

28 Where can we go up? Our brethren have discouraged our hearts, saying, "The people are greater and taller than we; the cities are great and built up to heaven; moreover we have seen the sons of the Anakim there."'

29 "Then I said to you, 'Do not be in awe, or afraid of them.

30 The Lord your God, who goes before you, He will fight for you, according to all He did for you in Egypt before your eyes, 31 and in the desert where you saw how the Lord your God carried you, as a man carries his son, in all the way that you went until you came to this place.'

32 Yet, after witnessing all of that, you still did not believe the Lord your God, 33 the one who went before you to search out a place for you to pitch your tents, in the fire by night and in the cloud by day, to show you the way to go.

Definitions

Wilderness
Word Definition:
An uninhabitable place
Contextual Definition:
Desert or deserted land
Substitution Word/phrase for clarity:
"desert"

Possess
Word Definition:
To own or take control of someone or something
Contextual Definition:
To take by force
Substitution Word/phrase for clarity:
"to take"

Scripture 5
Matthew 8:5-13 KJV

⁵ And when Jesus was entered into Capernaum, there came unto him a <u>centurion</u>, <u>beseeching</u> him, ⁶ Saying, Lord, my servant lieth at home sick of the palsy, <u>grievously</u> tormented.

⁷ And Jesus saith unto him, I will come and heal him.

⁸ The centurion answered and said, Lord, I am not worthy that thou shouldest come under my roof: but speak the word only, and my servant shall be healed.

⁹ For I am a man under authority, having soldiers under me: and I say to this man, Go, and he goeth; and to another, Come, and he cometh; and to my servant, Do this, and he doeth it.

¹⁰ When Jesus heard it, he <u>marveled</u>, and said to them that followed, Verily I say unto you, I have not found so great faith, no, not in Israel.

¹¹ And I say unto you, That many shall come from the east and west, and shall sit down with Abraham, and Isaac, and Jacob, in the kingdom of heaven.

¹² But the children of the kingdom shall be cast out into outer darkness: there shall be weeping and <u>gnashing</u> of teeth.

¹³ And Jesus said unto the centurion, Go thy way; and as thou hast believed, so be it done unto thee. And his servant was healed in the selfsame hour.

Matthew 8:5-13 Clarification

⁵ And when Jesus entered Capernaum, a centurion came to Him, begging Him, ⁶ saying, "Lord, my servant is lying at home with palsy, severely tormented."

⁷ And Jesus said to him, "I will come and heal him."

⁸ The centurion answered and said, "Lord, I am not worthy that You should come under my roof. But only speak a word, and my servant will be healed.

⁹ For I also am a man under authority, having soldiers under me.

And I say to this man, 'Go,' and he goes; and to another, 'Come,' and he comes; and to my servant, 'Do this,' and he does it."

[10] When Jesus heard it, He was excited, and said to those who followed, "Assuredly, I say to you, I have not found such great faith, not even in Israel!

[11] And I say to you that many will come from the east and west, and sit down with Abraham, Isaac, and Jacob in the kingdom of heaven.

[12] But the sons of the kingdom will be cast out into outer darkness. There will be weeping and grinding of teeth."

[13] Then Jesus said to the centurion, "Go your way; and as you have believed, so let it be done for you." And his servant was healed that same hour.

Definitions

Centurion
Word Definition:
A Roman solider commander in charge of one hundred soldiers
Contextual Definition:
A Roman solider commander in charge of one hundred soldiers
Substitution Word/phrase for clarity:
"Centurion"

Beseeching
Word Definition:
To beg or to urgently ask someone to do something
Contextual Definition:
To beg someone
Substitution Word/phrase for clarity:
"begging"

Grievously
Word Definition:
To have severe pain; to suffer; to have sorrow
Contextual Definition:
Severe pain, suffering, or sorrow
Substitution Word/phrase for clarity:
"severely"

Marvelled
Word Definition:
To wonder; To show astonishment or excitement
Contextual Definition:
Be shocked by extreme happiness or awe
Substitution Word/phrase for clarity:
"Excited"

Gnashing
Word Definition:
To grind your teeth together
Contextual Definition:
To grind your teeth together
Substitution Word/phrase for clarity:
"Grinding"

Scripture 6
Matthew 14:22-33 KJV

22And straightway Jesus constrained his disciples to get into a ship, and to go before him unto the other side, while he sent the multitudes away.
23And when he had sent the multitudes away, he went up into a mountain apart to pray: and when the evening was come, he was there alone.
24But the ship was now in the midst of the sea, tossed with waves: for the wind was contrary.
25And in the fourth watch of the night Jesus went unto them, walking on the sea.
26 And when the disciples saw him walking on the sea, they were troubled, saying, It is a spirit; and they cried out for fear.
27 But straightway Jesus spake unto them, saying, Be of good cheer; it is I; be not afraid.

28 And Peter answered him and said, Lord, if it be thou, bid me come unto thee on the water.
29 And he said, Come. And when Peter was come down out of the ship, he walked on the water, to go to Jesus.
30 But when he saw the wind boisterous, he was afraid; and beginning to sink, he cried, saying, Lord, save me.
31 And immediately Jesus stretched forth his hand, and caught him, and said unto him, O thou of little faith, wherefore didst thou doubt?
32 And when they were come into the ship, the wind ceased.
33 Then they that were in the ship came and worshiped him, saying, Of a truth thou art the Son of God.

Matthew 14:22-33 Clarification

22 Jesus specifically ordered his disciples to leave without him to the other side while he dispersed the crowd.

23 after the crowd dispersed, Jesus went to the mountain by himself and prayed until the evening.

24 by evening time, his disciples were caught up in a storm where the winds kept blowing against the ship.
25 Between 3am and 6am, Jesus walked to them on the sea.
26 The disciples thought Jesus was a spirit walking on the sea and cried out in fear.
27 Jesus immediately spoke to them saying, be of Good cheer; it's me; don't be afraid.
28 Peter responded to Jesus, saying if it's you, allow me to come to you on the water.
29 Jesus responded by saying "Come" and Peter got out of the ship and walked across the water towards Jesus.
30 Peter saw the winds severely increasing and became afraid and started to sink and cried out to Jesus Lord save me
31 And immediately Jesus stretched out his hand and grabbed him and said, O you of little faith, why did you doubt?
32 When Jesus and Peter made it back to the ship, the winds stopped.
33 The people in the ship came and worshiped Jesus saying he is truly the Son of God.

Definition

Straightway
Word Definition:
  Moving in a straight line
Contextual Definition:
  To be direct or something specifically to be done right away
Substitution Word/phrase for clarity:
  "Directly" or "Specifically"

Constrained
Word Definition:
  To be forced or controlled or restricted
Contextual Definition:
  To command someone to do something
Substitution Word/phrase for clarity:
  "Ordered"

Contrary
Word Definition:
  The opposite of something; The opposite direction
Contextual Definition:
  To be against one's direction

Substitution Word/phrase for clarity:
  "blowing against them"

Fourth Watch
Word Definition:
  N/A
Contextual Definition:
  The last watch of the night which is from 3am to 6am
Substitution Word/phrase for clarity:
  "Between 3:00 AM and 6:00AM"

Boisterous
Word Definition:
  Rowdy; Wild; Loud; Overexcited; Rough
Contextual Definition:
  To be overwhelming and loud; frightening
Substitution Word/phrase for clarity:
  "severely increase"

Scripture 7
Philippians 4:10-20 KJV

10 But I rejoiced in the Lord greatly, that now at the last your care of me hath flourished again; wherein ye were also careful, but ye lacked opportunity.

11 Not that I speak in respect of want: for I have learned, in whatsoever state I am, therewith to be content.

12 I know both how to be abased, and I know how to abound: every where and in all things I am instructed both to be full and to be hungry, both to abound and to suffer need.

13 I can do all things through Christ which strengtheneth me.

14 Notwithstanding ye have well done, that ye did communicate with my affliction.

15 Now ye Philippians know also, that in the beginning of the gospel, when I departed from Macedonia, no church communicated with me as concerning giving and receiving, but ye only.

16 For even in Thessalonica ye sent once and again unto my necessity.

17 Not because I desire a gift: but I desire fruit that may abound to your account.

18 But I have all, and abound: I am full, having received of Epaphroditus the things which were sent from you, an odour of a sweet smell, a sacrifice acceptable, wellpleasing to God.

19 But my God shall supply all your need according to his riches in glory by Christ Jesus.

20 Now unto God and our Father be glory for ever and ever. Amen.

Philippians 4:10-20 Clarification

10 But I rejoiced in the Lord greatly now that you started to care for me again; even though you didn't have the opportunity, I know you did care for me.

11 although I do not seek being cared for because I learned to be content in all things: 12 I know how to be devalued, and how to be powerful. I

have learned to be full and hungry, to be exalted and suffer.

13 I can do all things through Christ who strengthens me.

14 Nevertheless you have done well being that you shared in my trouble.

15 Now you Philippians recall the beginning of the gospel, when I departed from Macedonia, no church agreed with me about giving and receiving but you.

16 For even in Thessalonica you sent aid once and again for my necessities.

17 Not because I seek the gift, but I seek the fruit that flourishes from it.

18 Indeed I have what I need and prosper. I am full from what you sent me through Epaphroditus, a sweet-smelling aroma, an acceptable sacrifice that is well pleasing to God.

19 But my God shall supply all of your needs according to God's riches, by the exalted Jesus the Christ.

20 Now to our God and Father be the glory forever and ever. Amen.

Definition

Abased

Word Definition:
To belittle, lower, reduce, or degrade someone

Contextual Definition:
Make lower in value or status

Substitution Word/phrase for clarity:
"devalued"

Abound (Verse 12)

Word Definition:
Large in number or amount; to be plentiful

Contextual Definition:
To be powerful or have great influence

Substitution Word/phrase for clarity:
"powerful"

Affliction

Word Definition:
To cause pain, suffering, grief, or illness

Contextual Definition:
Circumstance that causes anxiety or hardship

Substitution Word/phrase for clarity:
"trouble"

Abound (Verse 17)

Word Definition:
Large in number or amount; to be plentiful

Contextual Definition:
To show great return or to flourish

Substitution Word/phrase for clarity:
"flourish"

Chapter 1 Activities

Complete the following passages by picking the correct word from the Word List below. Then find the words in the word-search puzzle on the next page.

Word List:
A. Stripes   B. Content   C. Immediately   D. Wilderness   E. Faith   F. Believe
G. Healed   H. Wounded   I. Good   J. Jesus   K. Christ   L. Strengthen

1. And we know that all things work together for _____ to them that love God, to them who are the called according to his purpose. (Romans 8:28 KJV) [Reading: Romans 8:18-30]

2. But He was _____ for our transgressions, He was bruised for our iniquities; The chastisement for our peace was upon Him, and by His _____ we are healed. (Isaiah 53:5 KJV) [Reading: Isaiah 53]

3. O love the Lord, all ye his saints: for the Lord preserveth the faithful, and plentifully rewardeth the proud doer. Be of good courage, and he shall _____ your heart, all ye that hope in the Lord. (Psalm 31:23-24 KJV) [Reading: Psalm 31]

4. And in the _____, where thou hast seen how that the Lord thy God bare thee, as a man doth bear his son, in all the way that ye went, until ye came into this place. Yet in this thing ye did not _____ the Lord your God, Who went in the way before you, to search you out a place to pitch your tents in, in fire by night, to shew you by what way ye should go, and in a cloud by day. (Deuteronomy 1:31-33 KJV) [Reading: Deuteronomy 1:19-33]

5. And _____ said unto the centurion, Go thy way; and as thou hast believed, so be it done unto thee. And his servant was _____ in the selfsame hour. (Matthew 8:13 KJV) [Matthew 8:5-13]

6. And _____ Jesus stretched out His hand and caught him, and said to him, "O you of little _____ why did you doubt?" And when they got into the boat, the wind ceased. (Matthew 14:31-32 KJV) [Matthew 14:22-33]

7. Not that I speak in respect of want: for I have learned, in whatsoever state I am, therewith to be _____. I know both how to be abased, and I know how to abound: everywhere and in all things I am instructed both to be full and to be hungry, both to abound and to suffer need. I can do all things through _____ which strengtheneth me. (Philippians 4:11-13 KJV) [Reading: Philippians 4:10-20]

Find the missing words from the passages on the previous page in the word-search puzzle below.

Word List:

Stripes Content Immediately Wilderness Faith Believe

Healed Wounded Jesus Christ Strengthen Good

```
U  T  Q  E  B  Y  C  H  R  I  C  O  N  T  I
E  Z  C  I  L  A  E  D  I  H  H  S  O  S  A
S  N  T  B  Z  V  S  U  R  E  Y  U  U  D  T
U  O  X  I  E  T  U  I  N  A  R  I  P  E  S
S  H  J  E  S  U  S  S  T  M  N  E  D  O  Y
T  H  R  E  W  T  P  S  I  G  M  R  H  T  L
R  E  A  I  X  O  S  E  B  E  L  I  E  V  E
E  N  L  P  M  Y  B  N  K  J  W  I  A  O  R
N  D  U  F  Y  M  X  R  Y  O  P  M  L  O  N
G  G  O  O  D  K  E  E  S  U  N  M  E  D  E
T  B  I  I  X  H  M  D  M  T  P  E  D  F  S
H  E  L  T  G  U  E  L  I  K  R  D  A  W  S
E  M  M  H  S  D  X  I  H  A  J  I  U  Q  K
N  I  G  E  N  I  T  W  A  I  T  A  P  Z  P
E  T  J  U  W  E  S  S  E  H  L  E  V  E  I
V  H  O  C  O  N  T  E  N  T  E  R  L  I  S
E  W  E  N  G  T  H  J  O  B  O  U  N  Y  T
```

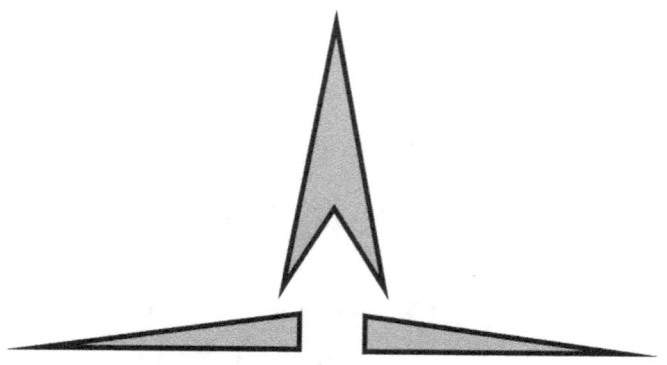

I believe in Jesus, I believe in God, I believe that my Lord died on the cross just for me. I believe that I am already healed, already saved, and already forgiven. I do not have to try to earn these things because there is nothing that I can do that will ever come close to earning what was given and restored to me by my God and my Lord. Healing, salvation, and forgiveness were given to me freely and freely I receive it. Thank you, my God and my Lord, for restoring me. Thank you, my God and my Lord, for loving me. Amen.

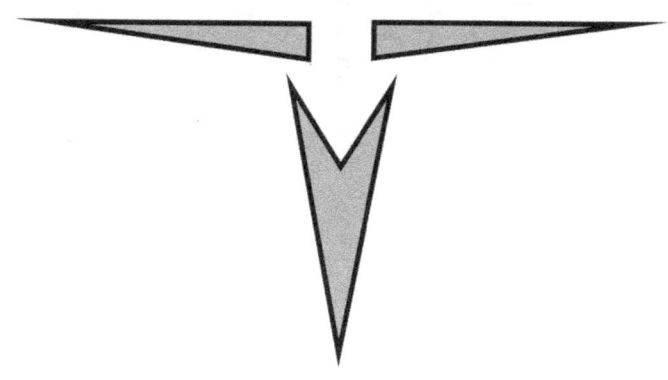

Chapter 2
Not What I Deserved, but What I Deserve

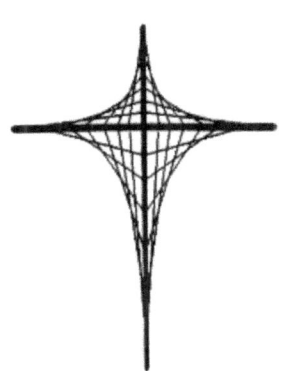

According to man's law, you must be punished when you do something wrong. And once you have been punished, you must carry that guilt and shame with you for the rest of your life. Included in this punishment is not being allowed to forget what you have done because it is added to your record and follows you around for the rest of your life. If man's law does not catch all of your wrong-doing, society will say that karma will 'get you' and make you pay for anything the law missed. As a believer of God living in this world, you must remember that you have accepted something that was made available to all of mankind... forgiveness. You have forgiveness for every bad thing you have done; Forgiveness for every bad thing you are doing; And forgiveness for every bad thing you will do. And with that forgiveness comes the freedom from judgment and guilt.

But why you? The reason is very simple: God loves you so much. God's love was the reason He sent Jesus to dwell among mankind to be an example; His example showed you how to live life with the authority God made available to all of mankind. God's love did not stop there; He wanted to wash away all of your wrongdoings and all of your sin. So He made Jesus the perfect sacrifice to pay the ultimate price for your sin once and for all. This was an everlasting sacrifice and it was done for every person on this earth, whether they believe in God or not. For every person on this earth, whether they love Him or not. For every person on this earth whether they are a Christian or not. Forgiveness was made available through Jesus' sacrifice to anyone who wants it; But only those who accepted Jesus as their Lord and Savior can take possession of it.

But, before you accepted Christ as your Lord and savior, you were not taking possession of this sacrifice nor all of the other things that were made available to you. However, when you accepted Christ as your Lord and savior, you took possession of all that Christ has made available for you and in doing so, you became a new creation that very second. This means that any sin or wrongdoing was washed away forever. Now, when God sees you, all he sees is his child, made perfect by the blood of his son Jesus. God does not see your sin, your faults, or your past because that was washed away through Jesus' blood. Christ's sacrifice and blood was more than enough to stop karma, spells, or curses and cover any sin or wrongdoing. And as an added benefit, God made available to you through Jesus: joy, peace, victory, prosperity, good health, and every good thing.

Always remember that you did not do anything to earn God's love, you did not do anything to deserve God's love, and you cannot do anything to lose God's love. The only parties involved in making these gifts available to you (through God's love) was God and Jesus, and not you. Everything that was done, was done before you even loved Him, before you even accepted Him, before you ever worshiped Him, and before you even came into this world. So just accept the fact that Jesus made it easy for you to receive all that was made available to you by God and be grateful!

Scripture 8
Zephaniah 3:9-20 KJV

9 For then will I turn to the people a pure language, that they may all call upon the name of the LORD, to serve him with one consent.

10 From beyond the rivers of Ethiopia my <u>suppliants</u>, even the daughter of my dispersed, shall bring mine offering.

11 In that day shalt thou not be ashamed for all thy doings, wherein thou hast <u>transgressed</u> against me: for then I will take away out of the midst of thee them that rejoice in thy pride, and thou shalt no more be <u>haughty</u> because of my holy mountain.

12 I will also leave in the midst of thee an afflicted and poor people, and they shall trust in the name of the LORD.

13 The remnant of Israel shall not do iniquity, nor speak lies; neither shall a deceitful tongue be found in their mouth: for they shall feed and lie down, and none shall make them afraid.

14 Sing, O daughter of Zion; shout, O Israel; be glad and rejoice with all the heart, O daughter of Jerusalem.

15 The LORD hath taken away thy judgments, he hath cast out thine enemy: the king of Israel, even the LORD, is in the midst of thee: thou shalt not see evil any more.

16 In that day it shall be said to Jerusalem, Fear thou not: and to Zion, Let not thine hands be slack.

17 The LORD thy God in the midst of thee is mighty; he will save, he will rejoice over thee with joy; he will rest in his love, he will joy over thee with singing.

18 I will gather them that are sorrowful for the <u>solemn</u> assembly, who are of thee, to whom the <u>reproach</u> of it was a burden.

19 Behold, at that time I will undo all that afflict thee: and I will save her that halteth, and gather her that was driven out; and I will get them praise and fame in every land where they have been put to shame.

20 At that time will I bring you again, even in the time that I gather you: for I will make you a name and a praise among all people of the earth, when I turn back your captivity before your eyes, saith the LORD.

Zephaniah 3:9-20 Clarification

9 I will return to the people a pure language, so that everyone can call upon the name of the LORD, and serve him as one.

10 From beyond the rivers of Ethiopia, my worshipers, even the daughters of my dispersed, shall bring me offerings.

11 On that day, you will not be ashamed of what you do, where you sinned against me: I will remove the people from you that rejoice in their own pride, and they will no longer be prideful because of my holy land.

12 I will leave you with the afflicted and poor, and they shall trust in the name of the LORD.

13 The remainder of Israel will not sin, nor speak lies; neither will they speak with a deceitful tongue: they will eat and rest, and nothing will make them afraid.

14 Sing, O daughter of Zion; shout, O Israel; be glad and rejoice with all of your heart, O daughter of Jerusalem.

15 The LORD has taken away your judgments, he cast out your enemy: the king of Israel, even the LORD, is in the middle of you: you will no longer see evil.

16 On that day, it will be said to Jerusalem, do not fear: and to Zion, do not let your hands fall down lifeless to your sides.

17 The LORD your God that is with you is mighty; he will save, he will rejoice over you with joy; he will rest in his love, he will rejoice over you with singing.

18 I will gather them that are hurt over the sacred assembly, those of you, to whom the disappointment of it was a burden.

19 Behold, at that time I will undo all that troubled you: and I will save them that quit, and gather them that was driven out; and I will give them praise and fame in every land in which they were put to shame.

20 At that time, I will once again show you, even in the time that I gather you: I will make you have honor and praise among all of people of the earth, as I reverse the effects of your captivity before your eyes, says the LORD.

Definitions

Suppliants
Word Definition:
>> Humble or sincere plea to someone

Definition:
>> A worshiper

Substitution Word/phrase for clarity:
>> "worshiper"

Transgressed
Word Definition:
>> To sin or violate a rule, law, or command

Contextual Definition:
>> Someone who sinned or is a sinner

Substitution Word/phrase for clarity:
>> "sin"

Haughty
Word Definition:
>> To behave arrogantly; prideful. Show dislike towards others viewed as inferior

Contextual Definition:
>> Acts superior, prideful and looking down on others

Substitution Word/phrase for clarity:
>> "prideful"

Solemn
Word Definition:
>> Enforcing religious beliefs

Contextual Definition:
>> Holy and sacred religious event

Substitution Word/phrase for clarity:
>> "sacred"

Reproach
Word Definition:
>> Disapproval or disappointment; Blame

Contextual Definition:
>> Disapproval or disappointment; Blame

Substitution Word/phrase for clarity:
>> "disappointment"

Scripture 9
2 Corinthians 5:1-21 KJV

This is part of a letter Paul wrote to the Corinthians.
See 2 Corinthians 2:14-7:1 for the entire letter.

¹ For we know that if our earthly house of this tabernacle were dissolved, we have a building of God, an house not made with hands, eternal in the heavens.

² For in this we groan, earnestly desiring to be clothed upon with our house which is from heaven:

³ If so be that being clothed we shall not be found naked.

⁴ For we that are in this tabernacle do groan, being burdened: not for that we would be unclothed, but clothed upon, that mortality might be swallowed up of life.

⁵ Now he that hath <u>wrought</u> us for the <u>selfsame</u> thing is God, who also hath given unto us the <u>earnest</u> of the Spirit.

⁶ Therefore we are always confident, knowing that, whilst we are at home in the body, we are absent from the Lord:

⁷ (For we walk by faith, not by sight:)

⁸ We are confident, I say, and willing rather to be absent from the body, and to be present with the Lord.

⁹ Wherefore we labour, that, whether present or absent, we may be accepted of him.

¹⁰ For we must all appear before the judgment seat of Christ; that every one may receive the things done in his body, according to that he hath done, whether it be good or bad.

¹¹ Knowing therefore the terror of the Lord, we persuade men; but we are made <u>manifest</u> unto God; and I trust also are made manifest in your consciences.

¹² For we <u>commend</u> not ourselves again unto you, but give you occasion to glory on our behalf, that ye may have somewhat to answer them which glory in appearance, and not in heart.

¹³ For whether we be beside ourselves, it is to God: or whether we be sober, it is for your cause.

14 For the love of Christ constraineth us; because we thus judge, that if one died for all, then were all dead:

15 And that he died for all, that they which live should not henceforth live unto themselves, but unto him which died for them, and rose again.

16 Wherefore henceforth know we no man after the flesh: yea, though we have known Christ after the flesh, yet now henceforth know we him no more.

17 Therefore if any man be in Christ, he is a new creature: old things are passed away; behold, all things are become new.

18 And all things are of God, who hath reconciled us to himself by Jesus Christ, and hath given to us the ministry of reconciliation;

19 To wit, that God was in Christ, reconciling the world unto himself, not imputing their trespasses unto them; and hath committed unto us the word of reconciliation.

20 Now then we are ambassadors for Christ, as though God did beseech you by us: we pray you in Christ's stead, be ye reconciled to God.

21 For he hath made him to be sin for us, who knew no sin; that we might be made the righteousness of God in him.

2 Corinthians 5:1-21 Clarification

1 For we know that if our earthly house of this tabernacle were dissolved, we have a building of God, an house not made with hands, eternal in the heavens.

2 Because of this, we grieve, and seriously desiring to be clothed with our house which is from heaven:

3 Being clothed, we will not be found naked.

4 We who are in this tabernacle do grieve, being burdened: not because we want to be unclothed, but clothed, that mortality might be swallowed up of life.

5 Now he who shaped us identical to God, who also gave us the best of the Spirit.

6 Therefore we are always confident in knowing that, while we are at home in this body, we are absent from the Lord: 7 (For we walk by faith, not by sight:)

⁸ We are confident, and rather be absent from the body, and to be present with the Lord.

⁹ Therefore we labor so that whether we are present or absent, we may be acceptable to him.

¹⁰ For we must all appear before the judgment seat of Christ; that everyone may be judged for the things done in their body, and receive according to what was done, whether it is good or bad.

¹¹ Knowing the terror of the Lord, we try to persuade men; but we are made clear to God; and I trust it is clear in your mind.

¹² We do not boast for you, we boast to give you an opportunity to boast on our behalf so you can tell them that only boast in appearance, and not in heart.

¹³ For whether we are beside ourselves, it is to God: or whether we are sober, it is for your cause.

¹⁴ For the love of Christ constrains us; because we judge, that if one died for all, then were all dead:

¹⁵ And Jesus died for all, so that every one who lives should not live for themselves, but live for Jesus who died for them, and rose again.

¹⁶ We no longer know any man after the flesh: but we once knew Christ after the flesh, but no longer.

¹⁷ Therefore if any man be in Christ, he is a new creature: old things are passed away; behold, all things have become new.

¹⁸ And all things are of God, who accepted us to himself by Jesus Christ, and given the ministry of restoration to us;

¹⁹ God was in Christ, restoring the world to himself, not counting their sin against them; and has given us the word of restoration.

²⁰ We are now ambassadors for Christ, God did beseech you through us: we pray you in Christ's place, restore yourself to God.

²¹ For God made Jesus to be sin for us, even though Jesus knew no sin; that we might be made the righteousness of God in him.

Definitions

Wrought
Word Definition:
> Molded or worked into a form in a deliberate way

Contextual Definition:
> Molded or worked into a form in a deliberate way

Substitution Word/phrase for clarity:
> "shape"

Selfsame
Word Definition:
> Being identical

Contextual Definition:
> Being identical

Substitution Word/phrase for clarity:
> "identical"

Earnest
Word Definition:
> Serious; Important; Great

Contextual Definition:
> The best of something

Substitution Word/phrase for clarity:
> "best"

Manifest
Word Definition:
> To detect using the senses; Detect by sight

Contextual Definition:
> To be made visibly clear

Substitution Word/phrase for clarity:
> "clear"

Commend
Word Definition:
> To be praised or glorified or noticed

Contextual Definition:
> To look highly upon or take pride in oneself

Substitution Word/phrase for clarity:
> "Praise"

Reconciled
Word Definition:
> To restore or resolve or accept something

Contextual Definition:
> To be accepted in spite of what was done

Substitution Word/phrase for clarity:
> "accepted"

Imputing
Word Definition:
> To give credit to someone; To assign something to a person, or group or movement

Contextual Definition:
> To count

Substitution Word/phrase for clarity:
> "counting"

Trespasses

Word Definition:
Mistake, Sin
Contextual Definition:
To commit sin
Substitution Word/phrase for clarity:
"sin"

Reconciliation

Word Definition:
To restore; setting or putting aside a dispute or disagreement
Contextual Definition:
To be made right in spite of what was done
Substitution Word/phrase for clarity:
"restoration"

Beseech

Word Definition:
To beg or to urgently ask someone to do something
Contextual Definition:
To beg or to urgently ask someone to do something
Substitution Word/phrase for clarity:
"beseech"

Stead

Word Definition:
A place; To act on someone's behalf
Contextual Definition:
Place
Substitution Word/phrase for clarity:
"place"

Scripture 10
Revelation 1:1-20 KJV

1 The Revelation of Jesus Christ, which God gave unto him, to shew unto his servants things which must shortly come to pass; and he sent and signified it by his angel unto his servant John: 2 Who bare record of the word of God, and of the testimony of Jesus Christ, and of all things that he saw.

3 Blessed is he that readeth, and they that hear the words of this prophecy, and keep those things which are written therein: for the time is at hand.

4 John to the seven churches which are in Asia: Grace be unto you, and peace, from him which is, and which was, and which is to come; and from the seven Spirits which are before his throne; 5 And from Jesus Christ, who is the faithful witness, and the first begotten of the dead, and the prince of the kings of the earth. Unto him that loved us, and washed us from our sins in his own blood, 6 And hath made us kings and priests unto God and his Father; to him be glory and dominion for ever and ever. Amen.

7 Behold, he cometh with clouds; and every eye shall see him, and they also which pierced him: and all kindreds of the earth shall wail because of him. Even so, Amen.

8 I am Alpha and Omega, the beginning and the ending, saith the Lord, which is, and which was, and which is to come, the Almighty.

9 I John, who also am your brother, and companion in tribulation, and in the kingdom and patience of Jesus Christ, was in the isle that is called Patmos, for the word of God, and for the testimony of Jesus Christ.

10 I was in the Spirit on the Lord's day, and heard behind me a great voice, as of a trumpet, 11 Saying, I am Alpha and Omega, the first and the last: and, What thou seest, write in a book, and send it unto the seven churches which are in Asia; unto Ephesus, and unto Smyrna, and unto Pergamos, and unto Thyatira, and unto Sardis, and unto Philadelphia, and unto Laodicea.

¹² And I turned to see the voice that spake with me. And being turned, I saw seven golden candlesticks; ¹³ And in the midst of the seven candlesticks one like unto the Son of man, clothed with a garment down to the foot, and girt about the paps with a golden girdle.

¹⁴ His head and his hairs were white like wool, as white as snow; and his eyes were as a flame of fire; ¹⁵ And his feet like unto fine brass, as if they burned in a furnace; and his voice as the sound of many waters.

¹⁶ And he had in his right hand seven stars: and out of his mouth went a sharp twoedged sword: and his countenance was as the sun shineth in his strength.

¹⁷ And when I saw him, I fell at his feet as dead. And he laid his right hand upon me, saying unto me, Fear not; I am the first and the last: ¹⁸ I am he that liveth, and was dead; and, behold, I am alive for evermore, Amen; and have the keys of hell and of death.

¹⁹ Write the things which thou hast seen, and the things which are, and the things which shall be hereafter; ²⁰ The mystery of the seven stars which thou sawest in my right hand, and the seven golden candlesticks. The seven stars are the angels of the seven churches: and the seven candlesticks which thou sawest are the seven churches.

Revelation 1:1-20 Clarification

¹ The Revelation of Jesus Christ, which was given to him by God, to show his servants the things that must come to pass shortly; and he sent and provided a sign through his angel to his servant John: ² Who will witness and record the word of God, and the testimony of Jesus Christ, and all the things that he saw.

³ Blessed is he that reads, and they that hear the words of this prophecy, and keep those things which are written therein: for the time is at hand.

⁴ John to the seven churches which are in Asia: Grace and peace to you, from him which is and which was and which is to come; and from the seven Spirits which are before his throne;

5 And from Jesus Christ, who is the faithful witness, and the first brought from the dead, and the prince of the kings of the earth. Unto him that loved us, and washed us from our sins in his own blood.

6 And made us kings and priests unto God and his Father; to him be the glory and dominion forever and ever. Amen

7 Behold, he comes with clouds; and everyone shall see him, including the ones who pierced him: and all made of the earth shall wail because of him. Amen.

8 I am the Alpha and Omega, the beginning and the ending, said the Lord, which is, and which was, and which is to come, the Almighty.

9 I John, who is also your brother, and partner in suffering, and in the kingdom and patience of Jesus Christ, was in the island that is called Patmos, for the word of God, and for the testimony of Jesus Christ.

10 I was in the Spirit on the Lord's day, and heard behind me a great voice, like a trumpet, 11 Saying, I am Alpha and Omega, the first and the last: and, Whatever you see, write it down in a book, and send it to the seven churches which are in Asia; to Ephesus, and to Smyrna, and to Pergamos, and to Thyatira, and to Sardis, and to Philadelphia, and to Laodicea.

12 And I turned to see the voice that spoke to me. And as I turned, I saw seven golden candlesticks; 13 And in the midst of the seven candlesticks was someone that resembled the Son of man, clothed with a garment down to the foot, and a wrap around the nipple with a golden girdle.

14 His head and his hairs were white like wool, as white as snow; and his eyes were as a flame of fire; 15 And his feet like unto fine brass, as if they burned in a furnace; and his voice as the sound of many waters.

16 And he had in his right hand seven stars: and out of his mouth went a sharp two-edged sword: and his appearance and composure was as the sun shines in his strength.

17 And when I saw him, I fell at his feet as dead. And he laid his right hand upon me, saying unto me, Fear not; I am the first and the last: 18 I am he that lives, and was dead; and, behold, I am alive forever, Amen; and have the keys of hell and of death.

[19] Write down what you saw, and the things which are now, and the things which are to come; [20] The mystery of the seven stars that you saw in my right hand, and the seven golden candlesticks. The seven stars are the angels of the seven churches: and the seven candlesticks that you saw are the seven churches.

Definitions

Signified
Word Definition:
To be expressed by a sign
Contextual Definition:
To give a physical sign to someone as confirmation
Substitution Word/phrase for clarity:
"provided a sign"

Begotten
Word Definition:
Offspring; Bring into existence
Contextual Definition:
To be brought forth
Substitution Word/phrase for clarity:
"brought"

Kindreds
Word Definition:
Family or related
Contextual Definition:
A group of people that come from the same place
Substitution Word/phrase for clarity:
"made"

Alpha
Word Definition:
First or Beginning
Contextual Definition:
The first or the start of something
Substitution Word/phrase for clarity:
"alpha"

Omega
Word Definition:
Last or End
Contextual Definition:
The last or end of something
Substitution Word/phrase for clarity:
"Omega"

Companion
Word Definition:
Associate or a mate
Contextual Definition:
Associate or a mate
Substitution Word/phrase for clarity:
"partner"

Tribulations
Word Definition:
Oppression; Suffering; Persecution; Trouble
Contextual Definition:
Oppression; Suffering; Persecution; Trouble
Substitution Word/phrase for clarity:
"suffering"

Isle
Word Definition:
A small Island
Contextual Definition:
A small island
Substitution Word/phrase for clarity:
"Island"

Girt
Word Definition:
To secure with a band or belt
Contextual Definition:
To secure with a band or belt
Substitution Word/phrase for clarity:
"wrap"

Paps
Word Definition:
Nipple
Contextual Definition:
Nipple
Substitution Word/phrase for clarity:
"nipple"

Girdle
Word Definition:
Something that encircles the body
Contextual Definition:
An article of clothing encircling the body
Substitution Word/phrase for clarity:
"girdle"

Countenance
Word Definition:
Look, expression, appearance
Contextual Definition:
Appearance, composure and expression
Substitution Word/phrase for clarity:
"Appearance and composure"

<u>Scripture 11</u>
Galatians 2:11-21 KJV

11 But when Peter was come to Antioch, I <u>withstood</u> him to the face, because he was to be blamed.

12 For before that certain came from James, he did eat with the Gentiles: but when they were come, he withdrew and separated himself, fearing them which were of the circumcision.

13 And the other Jews <u>dissembled</u> likewise with him; insomuch that Barnabas also was carried away with their dissimulation.

14 But when I saw that they walked not uprightly according to the truth of the gospel, I said unto Peter before them all, If thou, being a Jew, livest after the manner of Gentiles, and not as do the Jews, why compellest thou the Gentiles to live as do the Jews?

15 We who are Jews by nature, and not sinners of the Gentiles,

16 Knowing that a man is not justified by the works of the law, but by the faith of Jesus Christ, even we have believed in Jesus Christ, that we might be justified by the faith of Christ, and not by the works of the law: for by the works of the law shall no flesh be justified.

17 But if, while we seek to be justified by Christ, we ourselves also are found sinners, is therefore Christ the minister of sin? God forbid.

18 For if I build again the things which I destroyed, I make myself a <u>transgressor</u>.

19 For I through the law am dead to the law, that I might live unto God.

20 I am crucified with Christ: nevertheless I live; yet not I, but Christ liveth in me: and the life which I now live in the flesh I live by the faith of the Son of God, who loved me, and gave himself for me.

21 I do not frustrate the grace of God: for if righteousness come by the law, then Christ is dead in vain.

Galatians 2:7-9 KJV
(Added verse for clarity and background)

7 But contrariwise, when they saw that the gospel of the uncircumcision was committed unto me, as the gospel of the circumcision was unto Peter;
8 (For he that wrought effectually in Peter to the apostleship of the circumcision, the same was mighty in me toward the Gentiles:)
9 And when James, Cephas, and John, who seemed to be pillars, perceived the grace that was given unto me, they gave to me and Barnabas the right hands of fellowship; that we should go unto the heathen, and they unto the circumcision.

Galatians 2:11-21 Clarification

11 But when Peter was come to Antioch, I rejected him to the face, because he was to be blamed.
12 Before people associated with James came to town, Cephas ate with the Gentiles: But when they arrived, Cephas began to draw away and separated himself from the Gentiles because he was afraid of those who belonged to the circumcision group.
13 And the other Jews became hypocrites with him; so much that Barnabas also joined in their hypocrisy.
14 But when I saw that they did not walk according to the truth of the gospel, I said to Peter in front of all of them, If you, being a Jew, live as the Gentiles, and do not live as the Jews, then why make the Gentiles live as the Jews?
15 We who are Jews by nature, and not sinners of the Gentiles,
16 knowing that a person is not justified by the works of the law, but by faith in Jesus Christ. We also have to put our faith in Christ Jesus that we may be justified by faith in Christ and not by the works of the law, because no one is justified by the works of the law.
17 "But if, while seeking to be justified through Christ, we find

56

ourselves among the sinners, doesn't that mean that Christ promotes sin? No.

18 For if I rebuild the things that I destroyed, then I really am a sinner. **20** I have been crucified with Christ and but I live. It's not me who lives, but Christ who lives in me. The life I now live in the body, I live by faith in the Son of God, who loved me and gave himself for me.

21 I do not frustrate the grace of God, for if righteousness could be gained through the law, Christ died in vain.

<u>Definitions</u>

Withstood
Word Definition:
To stand up against; Resist or oppose
Contextual Definition:
To stand up against; Resist or oppose
Substitution Word/phrase for clarity:
"rejected"

Dissembled
Word Definition:
To deceive or hide the truth
Contextual Definition:
To deceive or hide the truth
Substitution Word/phrase for clarity:
"hypocrites"/"hypocrisy"

Transgressor
Word Definition:
To sin or violate a rule, law, or command
Contextual Definition:
To break a law or not follow a command
Substitution Word/phrase for clarity:
"sinner"

Scripture 12
Psalms 103 KJV

1 Bless the Lord, O my soul: and all that is within me, bless his holy name.

2 Bless the Lord, O my soul, and forget not all his benefits: 3 Who forgiveth all thine iniquities; who healeth all thy diseases; 4 Who redeemeth thy life from destruction; who crowneth thee with lovingkindness and tender mercies;

5 Who satisfieth thy mouth with good things; so that thy youth is renewed like the eagle's.

6 The Lord executeth righteousness and judgment for all that are oppressed.

7 He made known his ways unto Moses, his acts unto the children of Israel.

8 The Lord is merciful and gracious, slow to anger, and plenteous in mercy.

9 He will not always chide: neither will he keep his anger for ever.

10 He hath not dealt with us after our sins; nor rewarded us according to our iniquities.

11 For as the heaven is high above the earth, so great is his mercy toward them that fear him.

12 As far as the east is from the west, so far hath he removed our transgressions from us.

13 Like as a father pitieth his children, so the Lord pitieth them that fear him.

14 For he knoweth our frame; he remembereth that we are dust.

15 As for man, his days are as grass: as a flower of the field, so he flourisheth.

16 For the wind passeth over it, and it is gone; and the place thereof shall know it no more.

17 But the mercy of the Lord is from everlasting to everlasting upon them that fear him, and his righteousness unto children's children; 18 To such as keep his covenant, and to those that remember his commandments to do them.

19 The Lord hath prepared his throne in the heavens: and his kingdom ruleth over all.

20 Bless the Lord, ye his angels, that excel in strength, that do his commandments, hearkening unto the voice of his word.

21 Bless ye the Lord, all ye his <u>hosts</u>; ye ministers of his, that do his pleasure.

22 Bless the Lord, all his works in all places of his dominion: bless the Lord, O my soul.

Psalms 103 Clarification

1 Bless the Lord, O my soul: and all that is within me, bless his holy name: 2 Bless the Lord, O my soul, and forget not all his benefits: 3 Who forgives all your sins; who heals all your diseases; 4 Who saved your life from destruction; who crowns you with loving kindness and tender mercies; 5 Who satisfies your mouth with good things; so that your youth is renewed like the eagle's.

6 The Lord executes righteousness and judgment for all that are oppressed.

7 He made his ways known to Moses, and his actions to the children of Israel.

8 The Lord is merciful and gracious, slow to anger, and has plenty of mercy.

9 He will not always speak out in anger: neither will he keep his anger forever.

10 There is no need for him to deal with us because of our sins; nor reward us according to our sins.

11 For as high as the heaven is above the earth, so great is his mercy toward them that fear him.

12 As far as the east is from the west, so far has he removed our wrongdoing from us.

13 Like a father that feels sorrow for the pain of his children, so the Lord feels sorrow for the pain of them that fear him.

14 For he knows our frame; he remembers that we are dust.

15 As for man, his days are as grass: as a flower of the field, so he flourish.

16 For the wind passes over it, and it is gone; and the place thereof shall know it no more.

17 But the mercy of the Lord is from everlasting to everlasting to them that fear him, and his righteousness to children's children; 18 To those that keep his covenant, and to those that remember to do his commandments.

19 The Lord has prepared his throne in the heavens; and his kingdom rules over all.

20 Bless the Lord, you his angels that excel in strength, that do his commandments, and listens to the voice of his word.

21 Bless the Lord, all of you that are his vessels; the ministers of his, and that do his pleasure.

22 Bless the Lord, all his works in all places of his dominion: bless the Lord, O my soul.

Definitions

Iniquities
Word Definition:
Immoral behavior or actions; wickedness; an extreme injustice
Contextual Definition:
Sins
Substitution Word/phrase for clarity:
"Sins"

Redeemeth
Word Definition:
To be saved from any faults or consequences by a form of payment; Cleared
Contextual Definition:
To save something
Substitution Word/phrase for clarity:
"saved"

Mercies
Word Definition:
Favor or compassion
Contextual Definition:
Blessings, good fortune, special treatment, or compassion that is in your favor
Substitution Word/phrase for clarity:
"Mercies"

Plenteous
Word Definition:
Fruitful
Contextual Definition:
Plenty
Substitution Word/phrase for clarity:
"Plenty of"

Chide
Word Definition:
To chastise, berate or rebuke
Contextual Definition:
To speak out in anger
Substitution Word/phrase for clarity:
"speak out in anger"

Transgression
Word Definition:
To sin or violated a rule, law, or command
Contextual Definition:
Violation of a law
Substitution Word/phrase for clarity:
"wrongdoing"

Pitieth
Word Definition:
Sympathy or compassion for someone suffering
Contextual Definition:
Sympathy or compassion for someone suffering
Substitution Word/phrase for clarity:
"feels sorrow for the pain"

Frame
Word Definition:
Figure or physique of an animal or human body
Contextual Definition:
Figure or physique of an animal or human body
Substitution Word/phrase for clarity:
"frame"

Hosts
Word Definition:
A person or place that entertains or welcomes guests
Contextual Definition:
To provide a place for something or someone else like a vessel
Substitution Word/phrase for clarity:
"vessel"

Scripture 13
John 10:7-21 KJV

7 Then said Jesus unto them again, <u>Verily</u>, verily, I say unto you, I am the door of the sheep.

8 All that ever came before me are thieves and robbers: but the sheep did not hear them.

9 I am the door: by me if any man enter in, he shall be saved, and shall go in and out, and find pasture.

10 The thief cometh not, but for to steal, and to kill, and to destroy: I am come that they might have life, and that they might have it more abundantly.

11 I am the good shepherd: the good shepherd giveth his life for the sheep.

12 But he that is an <u>hireling</u>, and not the shepherd, whose own the sheep are not, seeth the wolf coming, and leaveth the sheep, and fleeth: and the wolf catcheth them, and scattereth the sheep.

13 The hireling fleeth, because he is an hireling, and careth not for the sheep.

14 I am the good shepherd, and know my sheep, and am known of mine.

15 As the Father knoweth me, even so know I the Father: and I lay down my life for the sheep.

16 And other sheep I have, which are not of this <u>fold</u>: them also I must bring, and they shall hear my voice; and there shall be one fold, and one shepherd.

17 Therefore doth my Father love me, because I lay down my life, that I might take it again.

18 No man taketh it from me, but I lay it down of myself. I have power to lay it down, and I have power to take it again. This commandment have I received of my Father.

19 There was a division therefore again among the Jews for these sayings.

20 And many of them said, He hath a devil, and is mad; why hear ye him?

21 Others said, These are not the words of him that hath a devil. Can a devil open the eyes of the blind?

John 10:7-21 Clarification

7 Then Jesus said to them again, In truth, I say to you, I am the door for the sheep.

8 All that ever came before me are thieves and robbers: but the sheep did not hear them.

9 I am the door: by me if any man enters, he will be saved, and go in and out, and find pasture.

10 The thief comes to steal, and to kill, and to destroy: I have come that they might have life, and that they might have it more abundantly.

11 I am the good shepherd: the good shepherd who gives his life for the sheep.

12 But he who is the hired help, and not the shepherd, and does not own the sheep, sees the wolf coming, and leaves the sheep, and flees: and the wolf catches them, and scatters the sheep.

13 The hired help flees because he is payed to be there and does not care about the sheep.

14 I am the good shepherd; and I know My own sheep, and I am known by them.

15 As the Father knows Me, I know the Father; and I lay down My life for the sheep.

16 And other sheep I have which are not of this covenant; I must bring them as well, and they will hear My voice; and there will be one covenant and one shepherd.

17 "Therefore My Father loves me, because I lay down my life that I may take it again.

18 No one can take my life from me, but I lay it down myself. I have power to lay it down, and I have power to take it again. This command I have received from my Father."

19 Therefore there was a division again among the Jews because of what Jesus said.

20 And many of them said, "He has a demon and is mad. Why do you listen to Him?"

21 Others said, "These are not the words of one who has a demon. Can a demon open the eyes of the blind?"

Definitions

Verily

Dictionary Definition:
To speak confidently in truth

Contextual Definition:
To say without any doubt

Substitution Word/phrase for clarity:
"Total certainty"

Hireling

Dictionary Definition:
A person who works purely for material reward.

Contextual Definition:
A person with selfish intentions but presents themselves as something more. Self-serving or hired help with no connection or loyalty to what they protect

Substitution Word/phrase for clarity:
"hired help"/"payed to be there"

Fold

Dictionary Definition:
A group of people or an institution that share a common faith, belief, activity, or enthusiasm

Contextual Definition:
Belonging to a covenant or agreement

Substitution Word/phrase for clarity:
"Covenant"

Chapter 2 Activities

Complete the following passages by picking the correct word from the Word List below. Then find the words in the word-search puzzle on the next page.

Word List:
A. Abundantly   B. Mighty   C. Rejoice   D. Righteousness   E. Reconciled   F. Transgressions

G. Become   H. Blood   I. Door   J. West   K. Faithful   L. Faith   M. Christ

1. The Lord thy God in the midst of thee is _____; he will save, he will _____ over thee with joy; he will rest in his love, he will joy over thee with singing (Zephaniah 3:17 KJV) [Reading: Zephaniah 3:9-20]

2. Therefore if any man be in Christ, he is a new creature: old things are passed away; behold, all things are _____ new (2 Corinthians 5:17 KJV) [Reading: 2 Corinthians 5:1-21]

3. And from Jesus Christ, who is the _____ witness, and the first begotten of the dead, and the prince of the kings of the earth. Unto him that loved us, and washed us from our sins in his own _____. (Revelation 1:5 KJV) [Reading: Revelation 1:1-20]

4. Now then we are ambassadors for _____, as though God did beseech you by us: we pray you in Christ's stead, be ye _____ to God (2 Corinthians 5:20 KJV) [Reading: 2 Corinthians 5:1-21]

5. I am crucified with Christ: nevertheless I live; yet not I, but Christ liveth in me: and the life which I now live in the flesh I live by the _____ of the Son of God, who loved me, and gave himself for me. I do not frustrate the grace of God: for if _____ come by the law, then Christ is dead in vain (Galatians 2:20-21 KJV) [Reading: Galatians 2:11-21]

6. As far as the East is from the _____, so far hath he removed our _____ from us (Psalm 103:12 KJV) [Reading: Psalm 103]

7. I am the _____: by me if any man enter in, he shall be saved, and shall go in and out, and find pasture. The thief cometh not, but for to steal, and to kill, and to destroy: I am come that they might have life, and that they might have it more _____. (John 10:9-10 KJV) [Reading: John 10:7-21]

Find the missing words from the passages in the word-search puzzle below.

Word List:
Abundantly Mighty Rejoice Righteousness Reconciled Transgressions

Become Blood Door Faithful Faith Christ West

```
A D M F R D R T T R B T A S S W B
O R W O N B E C O M E D C N G D J
D R I M I O L R W T R S F O Z B L
O E F A T I G H T Q R W M I G H T
W C T O R V J Y K Z R Q G S G J D
D O B J Q R Q U L B I C S S W Q H
Y N K E T W A R N T O E B E N D N
T C F M Z C E B L P N G J R C R E
Q I Y I N T R A N S E A F G U B S
U L W G Q D J F U N Z T D S R E S
T E G H C O M O O D J N Q N F I W
C D Z T C X E D A A I T H A U Z K
B D W Y B T D W F R I S C R W B Y
F A I T H F U L Q B U N R T O I A
C R R G C W O E T A J E O R A F Y
T R I W B E B E C W A D B L W D O
W R R B I R F D E R F A I T H G I
U N X G K B D W F F C U N C Z A T
O C E A L T I B W B R J P X Y U N
V L D B L O O D Q E Y G W V Z L D
S I L J Y Y Z O J S B T X V U E S
N F R U X A T O Q R V P G H A O T
V W I S G W I R Q N D A M J N L E
T E A E T C H R I S T L V K K D T
Z S D K E J G C H G E C A I G J X
Y T X V F F E B D Q H D C L B A Z
R B S G R A C G L R B U N J O I E
N A R T W A R R I O R A F E C E W
S X A B U D I G F M I G H R I G H
```

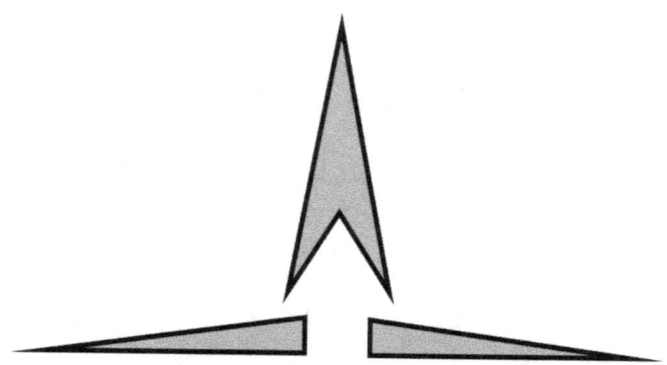

Jesus, I thank you for your love. Heavenly father, I thank you for your love. You loved me so much that you saved me, sanctified me, and delivered me from a lifetime of sin. You washed away my past and made me brand new. Through you, the trials of life will never last, and only goodness and mercy will follow me all the days of my life. Amen

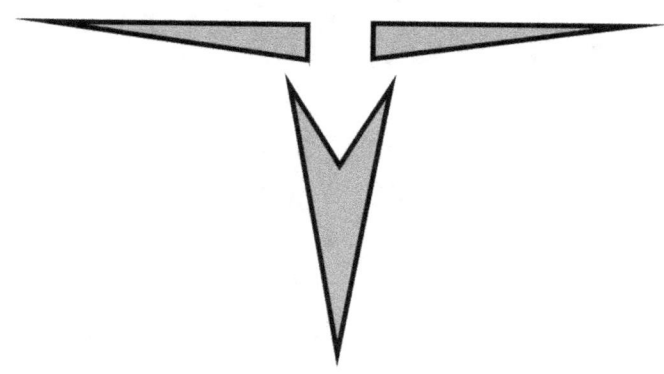

Chapter 3
Be Encouraged

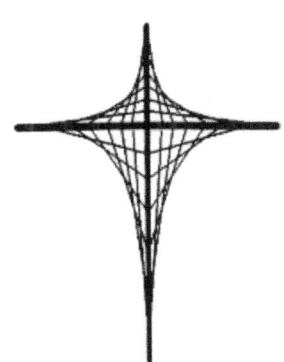

Even in your darkest hour, when all seems lost, you feel all alone, and you can't seem to find your way out or know how you will make it through...be encouraged. Whatever darkness is around you, whatever situation you are in, wherever you may be right now, always remember that you serve an awesome God and that this awesome God will see you through.

Always remember that "making it through" is not the same as "not going through." Remembering this difference is important because the enemy will want you to confuse the two in order to uproot your faith. Remember "making it through" means that you are already in your situation. "Not going though" simply means that you are not in a troubling situation or that whatever is coming your way is still avoidable.

The enemy's goal is to wear you down by any means necessary. The enemy will try to get you to fight when there is nothing to fight and not fight when you should be fighting. The enemy's end goal is to win the fight by either making you too tired to fight or so passive that you don't even want to fight.

hen you are believing God to strengthen you for a fight that does not exist, nothing will happen. When you are believing God to prevent a fight from happening while you are in the middle of the fight, nothing will happen. He simply cannot answer your cry because you are asking Him to do something that does not make any sense. The enemy knows this and that will provide the perfect opportunity for the enemy to introduce some doubt into your life. Doubt you are good enough or prayed hard enough, shouted hard enough, went to church enough, or gave enough. If you find yourself facing that doubt, always remember, there was nothing that you did to earn God's love and there is nothing you can do or not do that will cause you to lose it. Jesus is the reason for all the good in your life; do not try to take credit for something that He did for you. In spite of all your flaws, He loved you and He died for you so you can be acceptable to God.

ome things in this life can be avoided while other things will require you to go through them in order to make it to the other side stronger and wiser. Stay in prayer and listen because the wisdom of God will always tell you which is which. So, whenever a situation cannot be avoided and you are left to fight, you fight with God on your side. This is powerful because God has never lost a battle and you will always come out on top. And when the situation calls for you to wait or avoid it, simply rest in God's perfect peace. This is wonderful because God's level of peace goes beyond all understanding. It will confuse the world to see you in such perfect peace while you are in the midst of your trouble.

he only person who can stop God's intervention from happening is you, because God gave you free will: You can choose to stop fighting, you can choose to rehearse all the stories you have heard of people not making it out of similar situations, you can choose to give up when it gets tough or worse...do nothing, or you can give in when your body feels weak. So, when the only person who can stop you is you, and you choose to lean on God and not quit: God will tell you which way to go; God will give you strength when you need to keep on fighting; God will surround you with His presence when you need comfort; and God will send His word when you need restoration. So, always remember, no matter what is going on, you are destined to win. You will win because you serve a mighty God and a powerful Lord, and they both love you.

Scripture 14
Romans 14:1-13 KJV

¹ Him that is weak in the faith receive ye, but not to doubtful disputations.

² For one believeth that he may eat all things: another, who is weak, eateth herbs.

³ Let not him that eateth despise him that eateth not; and let not him which eateth not judge him that eateth: for God hath received him.

⁴ Who art thou that judgest another man's servant? to his own master he standeth or falleth. Yea, he shall be holden up: for God is able to make him stand.

⁵ One man esteemeth one day above another: another esteemeth every day alike. Let every man be fully persuaded in his own mind.

⁶ He that regardeth the day, regardeth it unto the Lord; and he that regardeth not the day, to the Lord he doth not regard it. He that eateth, eateth to the Lord, for he giveth God thanks; and he that eateth not, to the Lord he eateth not, and giveth God thanks.

⁷ For none of us liveth to himself, and no man dieth to himself.

⁸ For whether we live, we live unto the Lord; and whether we die, we die unto the Lord: whether we live therefore, or die, we are the Lord's.

⁹ For to this end Christ both died, and rose, and revived, that he might be Lord both of the dead and living.

¹⁰ But why dost thou judge thy brother? or why dost thou set at nought thy brother? for we shall all stand before the judgment seat of Christ.

¹¹ For it is written, As I live, saith the Lord, every knee shall bow to me, and every tongue shall confess to God.

¹² So then every one of us shall give account of himself to God.

¹³ Let us not therefore judge one another any more: but judge this rather, that no man put a stumbling block or an occasion to fall in his brother's way.

Romans 14:1-13 Clarification

1 Accept someone who is weak in their faith, but not to argue about questionable things.

2 For one believes he may eat anything, but the other one who is weak believes he can only eat herbs.

3 The one who eats anything should not despise the one who believes he can't; the one who eats anything should not judge the one who believes he can't; God has accepted him.

4 Who are you to judge another's servant? It is up to his own master to decide if he stands or if he falls. He will be made to stand because God will be able to make him stand.

5 One person is exalted above another for one day; and another is exalted all the time above another. Let each one be confident in his own mind.

6 He who observes the day, observes it to the Lord; he who does not observe the day, to the Lord he does not observe it. He who eats anything, eats anything to the Lord, for he gives God thanks; He who does not eat anything, does not eat everything to the Lord, for he gives God thanks.

7 No one lives for themselves, and no one dies for themselves.

8 For if we live, we live to the Lord; and if we die, we die to the Lord. Therefore, whether we live or die, we are the Lord's.

9 For this is the reason Christ died and lived again, so that he will be Lord of both the dead and living.

10 So why do you judge your brother or sister? Or why do you show contempt for your brother or sister? For all of us will stand before the judgment seat of God.

11 For it is written:
"As I live, says the Lord,
Every knee shall bow to Me,
And every tongue shall confess to God."

12 So each of us shall give account of themselves to God.

13 Therefore let us stop judging each other, instead resolve it by not putting a stumbling block in our brother's way or bring up something that will cause them to fall.

Definitions

Esteemeth

Word Definition:
To be respected or highly valued

Contextual Definition:
To be lifted or exalted

Substitution Word/phrase for clarity:
"Exalted"

Scripture 15
2 Corinthians 1:3-11 KJV

3 Blessed be God, even the Father of our Lord Jesus Christ, the Father of mercies, and the God of all comfort;
4 Who comforteth us in all our tribulation, that we may be able to comfort them which are in any trouble, by the comfort wherewith we ourselves are comforted of God.
5 For as the sufferings of Christ abound in us, so our consolation also aboundeth by Christ.
6 And whether we be afflicted, it is for your consolation and salvation, which is effectual in the enduring of the same sufferings which we also suffer: or whether we be comforted, it is for your consolation and salvation.
7 And our hope of you is stedfast, knowing, that as ye are partakers of the sufferings, so shall ye be also of the consolation.
8 For we would not, brethren, have you ignorant of our trouble which came to us in Asia, that we were pressed out of measure, above strength, insomuch that we despaired even of life:
9 But we had the sentence of death in ourselves, that we should not trust in ourselves, but in God which raiseth the dead:
10 Who delivered us from so great a death, and doth deliver: in whom we trust that he will yet deliver us;
11 Ye also helping together by prayer for us, that for the gift bestowed upon us by the means of many persons thanks may be given by many on our behalf.

2 Corinthians 1:3-11 Clarification

3 Praise be to the God and Father of our Lord Jesus Christ, the Father of compassion and the God of all comfort, 4 who comforts us in all of our troubles, so that we can comfort those in any trouble with the same comfort that we received from God.
5 For as we share greatly in the suffering of Christ. our comfort flourishes through Christ.
6 If we are afflicted, it is for your comfort and salvation; if we are comforted, it is for your comfort,

which produces compassion for the same suffering that we suffer.

7 And our hope for you is firm, because we know you share in our suffering, so you will also share in our comfort.

8 brothers and sisters, we do not want you to be uninformed about the troubles we experienced in the province of Asia. We were under great pressure, far beyond our ability to endure, so that we lost all hope, even for life itself.

9 Indeed, we felt that we received the sentence of death. But this happened so we do not rely on ourselves but on God, who raises the dead.

10 He delivered us from such a deadly trial, and he will deliver us again. In him we have placed our hope that he will continue to deliver us, 11 you are also helping by praying for us. Then many will give thanks on our behalf for the gracious favor granted to us in the answered prayers of many.

<u>Definitions</u>

Abound
Word Definition:
Large in numbers or
amount; to be plentiful
Contextual Definition:
To show great return or to
flourish
Substitution Word/phrase for
clarity:
"flourish"

Despaired
Word Definition:
Hopelessness
Contextual Definition:
Hopelessness
Substitution Word/phrase for
clarity:
"lost hope"

Scripture 16
Jeremiah 17:1-13 KJV

1 The sin of Judah is written with a pen of iron, and with the point of a diamond: it is graven upon the table of their heart, and upon the horns of your altars;

2 Whilst their children remember their altars and their <u>groves</u> by the green trees upon the high hills.

3 O my mountain in the field, I will give thy substance and all thy treasures to the <u>spoil</u>, and thy high places for sin, throughout all thy borders.

4 And thou, even thyself, shalt discontinue from thine <u>heritage</u> that I gave thee; and I will cause thee to serve thine enemies in the land which thou knowest not: for ye have kindled a fire in mine anger, which shall burn for ever.

5 Thus saith the Lord; Cursed be the man that trusteth in man, and maketh flesh his <u>arm</u>, and whose heart departeth from the Lord.

6 For he shall be like the <u>heath</u> in the desert, and shall not see when good cometh; but shall inhabit the parched places in the wilderness, in a salt land and not inhabited.

7 Blessed is the man that trusteth in the Lord, and whose hope the Lord is.

8 For he shall be as a tree planted by the waters, and that spreadeth out her roots by the river, and shall not see when heat cometh, but her leaf shall be green; and shall not be careful in the year of drought, neither shall cease from yielding fruit.

9 The heart is deceitful above all things, and desperately wicked: who can know it?

10 I the Lord search the heart, I try the reins, even to give every man according to his ways, and according to the fruit of his doings.

11 As the partridge sitteth on eggs, and hatcheth them not; so he that getteth riches, and not by right, shall leave them in the midst of his days, and at his end shall be a fool.

12 A glorious high throne from the beginning is the place of our sanctuary.

13 O Lord, the hope of Israel, all that <u>forsake</u> thee shall be ashamed, and they that depart from me shall be

written in the earth, because they have forsaken the LORD, the fountain of living waters.

Jeremiah 17:1-13 Clarification

1 "Judah's sin is written with an iron pen; it is engraved with a diamond point on their heart, and on the horns of their altars, 2Their children remember their altars and their wooden images (of the goddess Asherah) by the green trees on the high hills.

3 On my mountain in the land [that I gave you], I will take your wealth and all of your treasures and give it away along with your high places of sin that are within all your borders.

4 Through your own fault, you will lose your inheritance which I gave you; and I will cause you to serve your enemies in a land which you do not know; For you have lit a fire with my anger which shall burn forever."

5 Thus says the Lord: "Cursed is the one who trusts in man and rely on their flesh for strength, whose heart departs from the Lord.

6 For he shall be like a shrub in the dessert, and shall not see when good comes, but shall live in the dry places of the wilderness, an inhabitable land.

7 "Blessed is the one who trusts in the Lord, and whose hope is the Lord.

8 For they will be like a tree planted by the water, whose roots spread out by the river, and will not fear when trouble comes; their leaves will be green, and will not be troubled in the year of drought, neither will they stop producing fruit.

9 "The heart is deceitful above all, and desperately weak; who can understand it?

10 The Lord searches the heart and the Lord tests now the heart will listen to Him, even to the point of giving to every man according to his ways, which is according to their actions.

11 "As a partridge bird that lays her eggs but nothing hatches, the same goes for the one who gets riches dishonestly; it will leave him during

his days on Earth, and at the end he will be made a fool."

12 A glorious high throne from the beginning and where our sanctuary is.

13 O Lord, the hope of Israel, all those who abandon you shall be ashamed. "Those who depart from me shall have their names written in the Earth, because they have abandoned the Lord, the fountain of living waters.

Definitions

Groves
Word Definition:
  N/A
Contextual Definition:
  An alter
Substitution Word/phrase for clarity:
  "alter"

Spoil
Word Definition:
  Pillage; Rob; Ruin
Contextual Definition:
  Take with violence; Rob; Pillage; Plunder
Substitution Word/phrase for clarity:
  "take"

Heritage
Word Definition:
  Possessions that go to an heir
Contextual Definition:
  A birthright or inheritance or honor that is passed down
Substitution Word/phrase for clarity:
  "Inheritance"

Arm
Word Definition:
  Power; Strength
Contextual Definition:
  Power, Strength, or might
Substitution Word/phrase for clarity:
  "strength"

Heath
Word Definition:
  A wasteland area
Contextual Definition:
  Especially flat, shrubby, desolate land
Substitution Word/phrase for clarity:
  "shrub"

Forsake
Word Definition:
  To renounce or give up or abandon or turn away
Contextual Definition:
  To renounce or give up or abandon or turn away
Substitution Word/phrase for clarity:
  "Abandon"

Scripture 17
Jeremiah 17:14-18 KJV

14 Heal me, O Lᴏʀᴅ, and I shall be healed; save me, and I shall be saved: for thou art my praise.

15 Behold, they say unto me, Where is the word of the Lᴏʀᴅ? let it come now.

16 As for me, I have not <u>hastened</u> from being a pastor to follow thee: neither have I desired the <u>woeful</u> day; thou knowest: that which came out of my lips was right before thee.

17 Be not a <u>terror</u> unto me: thou art my hope in the day of evil.

18 Let them be confounded that persecute me, but let not me be <u>confounded</u>: let them be <u>dismayed</u>, but let not me be dismayed: bring upon them the day of evil, and destroy them with double destruction.

Jeremiah 17:14-18 Clarification

14 Lord if you heal me, I will be healed; If you Save me, I will be saved, For You are the one that I will praise.

15 They keep saying to me, "Where is the word of the Lord? Let it come now!"

16 But for me, I am not quick to turn away from being your pastor, neither do I wish for any affliction; You my Lord know what I say; I did not hide it from you.

17 Do not be against me; Because you are my hope in the evil day.

18 Let the ones who persecute me be ashamed, But do not let me be put to shame; Let them be shaken, But do not let me be shaken. Bring on them the evil day, And destroy them with double destruction.

Definitions

Hastened

Word Definition:
To move or travel or proceed quickly

Contextual Definition:
To move or travel or proceed quickly

Substitution Word/phrase for clarity:
"quick"

Woeful [Day]

Word Definition:
Suffering, sorrow, unhappy, grievous

Contextual Definition:
Something dreadful, or sorrowful, or affliction that occurs

Substitution Word/phrase for clarity:
"Affliction"

Terror

Word Definition:
Violence or intense fear or intimidation

Contextual Definition:
Take an opposing stance or become an opponent

Substitution Word/phrase for clarity:
"against"

Confounded

Word Definition:
Confused, perplexed, annoyance

Contextual Definition:
Shame

Substitution Word/phrase for clarity:
"ashamed"

Dismayed

Word Definition:
Loss of courage or alarmed or fearful

Contextual Definition:
Feeling anxious or in distress due to fear

Substitution Word/phrase for clarity:
"Shaken"

<u>Scripture 18</u>
Psalm 107 KJV

¹ O give thanks unto the Lord, for he is good: for his mercy <u>endureth</u> for ever.

² Let the <u>redeemed</u> of the Lord say so, whom he hath redeemed from the hand of the enemy; ³ And gathered them out of the lands, from the east, and from the west, from the north, and from the south.

⁴ They wandered in the wilderness in a <u>solitary</u> way; they found no city to dwell in.

⁵ Hungry and thirsty, their soul fainted in them.

⁶ Then they cried unto the Lord in their trouble, and he delivered them out of their distresses.

⁷ And he led them forth by the right way, that they might go to a city of habitation.

⁸ Oh that men would praise the Lord for his goodness, and for his wonderful works to the children of men!

⁹ For he satisfieth the <u>longing</u> soul, and filleth the hungry soul with goodness.

¹⁰ Such as sit in darkness and in the shadow of death, being bound in affliction and iron;

¹¹ Because they rebelled against the words of God, and <u>contemned</u> the counsel of the most High:

¹² Therefore he brought down their heart with labour; they fell down, and there was none to help.

¹³ Then they cried unto the Lord in their trouble, and he saved them out of their distresses.

¹⁴ He brought them out of darkness and the shadow of death, and brake their bands in sunder.

¹⁵ Oh that men would praise the Lord for his goodness, and for his wonderful works to the children of men!

¹⁶ For he hath broken the <u>gates of brass</u>, and cut the bars of iron in <u>sunder</u>.

¹⁷ Fools because of their transgression, and because of their iniquities, are afflicted.

¹⁸ Their soul <u>abhorreth</u> all manner of meat; and they draw near unto the gates of death.

19 Then they cry unto the LORD in their trouble, and he saveth them out of their distresses.

20 He sent his word, and healed them, and delivered them from their destructions.

21 Oh that men would praise the LORD for his goodness, and for his wonderful works to the children of men!

22 And let them sacrifice the sacrifices of thanksgiving, and declare his works with rejoicing.

23 They that go down to the sea in ships, that do business in great waters;

24 These see the works of the LORD, and his wonders in the deep.

25 For he commandeth, and raiseth the stormy wind, which lifteth up the waves thereof.

26 They mount up to the heaven, they go down again to the depths: their soul is melted because of trouble.

27 They reel to and fro, and stagger like a drunken man, and are at their wit's end.

28 Then they cry unto the LORD in their trouble, and he bringeth them out of their distresses.

29 He maketh the storm a calm, so that the waves thereof are still.

30 Then are they glad because they be quiet; so he bringeth them unto their desired haven.

31 Oh that men would praise the LORD for his goodness, and for his wonderful works to the children of men!

32 Let them exalt him also in the congregation of the people, and praise him in the assembly of the elders.

33 He turneth rivers into a wilderness, and the watersprings into dry ground; 34 A fruitful land into barrenness, for the wickedness of them that dwell therein.

35 He turneth the wilderness into a standing water, and dry ground into watersprings.

36 And there he maketh the hungry to dwell, that they may prepare a city for habitation;

37 And sow the fields, and plant vineyards, which may yield fruits of increase.

38 He blesseth them also, so that they are multiplied greatly; and suffereth not their cattle to decrease.

[39] Again, they are minished and brought low through oppression, affliction, and sorrow.

[40] He poureth contempt upon princes, and causeth them to wander in the wilderness, where there is no way.

[41] Yet setteth he the poor on high from affliction, and maketh him families like a flock.

[42] The righteous shall see it, and rejoice: and all iniquity shall stop her mouth.

[43] Whoso is wise, and will observe these things, even they shall understand the lovingkindness of the LORD.

Psalm 107 Clarification

[1] Oh, give thanks to the Lord, for He is good! For His mercy lasts forever.

[2] Let those saved by the Lord say so, Whom He has rescued from the hand of the enemy, [3]And took them out of the lands, from the East and from the West, from the North, and from the South.

[4] They sorrowfully wandered in the wilderness; they did not find a city to live in.

[5] Hungry and thirsty, their soul fainted in them.

[6] Then they cried out to the Lord in their trouble, and He delivered them out of their distresses.

[7] And He led them the right way, so they might go to live in a city.

[8] So that mankind would give praise to the Lord for his goodness, and for his wonderful works to the children of men!

[9] For he satisfies the hungry soul, and fills the hungry soul with goodness.

[10] Those who sat in darkness and in the shadow of death, who live in affliction and irons chains.

[11] Because they rebelled against the words of God, and despised the counsel of the Most High, [12]He humbled them with labor and they fell with no one to help.

[13] Then they cried out to the Lord in their trouble, and He saved them from their distresses.

14 He brought them out of darkness and out of the shadow of death, and broke their chains into pieces.

15 So that mankind would give thanks to the Lord for his goodness, and for his wonderful works to the children of men!

16 For He has broken the gates made of brass and cut the iron bars in two.

17 The fools were afflicted because of their transgression, and because of their iniquities.

18 Their soul rejected all manner of food, and they came close to death.

19 Then they cried out to the Lord in their trouble, and He saved them from their distress.

20 He sent his word and healed them, and delivered them from their destructions.

21 So that mankind would give praise to the Lord for his goodness, and for his wonderful works to the Children of men.

22 For them that sacrifice, let their sacrifice be of Thanksgiving and declare His works with rejoicing.

23 Those who go down to the sea in ships, who do business on the great waters, 24 They see the works of the Lord, and His wonders in the deep.

25 For he commands and raises the stormy wind, which intensifies the waves of the sea.

26 Their ships mount up to the heavens, then their ships go down again to the depths; Their soul melts because of trouble.

27 They turn in opposite directions and stagger like a drunken man, and are at their wits' end.

28 Then they cry out to the Lord in their trouble, and He brings them out of their distresses.

29 He calms the storm, so the waves are still.

30 Then they are glad because of the quiet; So He guides them to their desired safe place.

31 So that mankind would give thanks to the Lord for his goodness, and for his wonderful works to the children of men!

32 Also let them exalt him in the assembly of the people, and praise him in the company of the elders.

33 He turns the habitable land by rivers into an uninhabitable land, and the springs of water into dry ground; 34 A fruitful land into a barren land, for the wickedness of those who live in it.

35 He turns a wilderness into pools of water and a dry land into springs of water.

36 There He brings the hungry so they may establish a city for a habitation, 37 and sow fields and plant vineyards, that they may produce a fruitful harvest.

38 He also blesses them and they multiply greatly; and he makes sure their cattle do not decrease.

39 When they are diminished and brought low through oppression, affliction, and sorrow, 40 He places contempt on princes, and causes them to wander in the wilderness where there is no way out; 41 Yet He sets the poor on high, far from affliction, and makes their families like a flock.

42 The righteous see it and rejoice, and all iniquity stops in its tracks.

43 Whoever is wise will observe these things, and they will understand the loving kindness of the Lord.

Definitions

Endureth
Word Definition:
   To continue without stopping
Contextual Definition:
   To never stop or fail
Substitution Word/phrase for clarity:
   "last"

Redeemed
Word Definition:
   To be saved from any faults or consequences by a form of payment; Cleared
Contextual Definition:
   To take back or rescue
Substitution Word/phrase for clarity:
   "Rescue"

Solitary
Word Definition:
   Being, living, or alone or hermit
Contextual Definition:
   Joyless, cheerless, and sorrowful through or as if through separation from a loved one
Substitution Word/phrase for clarity:
   "Sorrowful"

Longing
Word Definition:
   An intense desire
Contextual Definition:
   An intense desire
Substitution Word/phrase for clarity:
   "hungry"

Contemned
Word Definition:
   Scorn or despise
Contextual Definition:
   Scorn or despise
Substitution Word/phrase for clarity:
   "despises"

Gates of Brass
Word Definition:
   N/A
Contextual Definition:
   Strong gates that are reinforced and unbreakable
Substitution Word/phrase for clarity:
   "Gates of Brass"

Sunder
Word Definition:
To break apart or separate
Contextual Definition:
To break apart or separate
Substitution Word/phrase for clarity:
"two"

Abhorreth
Word Definition:
Hatred or disgust
Contextual Definition:
To reject or lose desire for
Substitution Word/phrase for clarity:
"reject"

Reel
Word Definition:
To turn or move around
Contextual Definition:
To turn or go around and around
Substitution Word/phrase for clarity:
"Turn"

To and Fro
Word Definition:
Continuous movements in opposite directions
Contextual Definition:
Continuous movements in opposite directions
Substitution Word/phrase for clarity:
"in opposite directions"

Haven
Word Definition:
A safe place
Contextual Definition:
A safe place
Substitution Word/phrase for clarity:
"safe place"

Scripture 19
Psalm 31 KJV

1 In thee, O Lord, do I put my trust; let me never be ashamed: deliver me in thy righteousness.

2 Bow down thine ear to me; deliver me speedily: be thou my strong rock, for an house of defence to save me.

3 For thou art my rock and my fortress; therefore for thy name's sake lead me, and guide me.

4 Pull me out of the net that they have laid privily for me: for thou art my strength.

5 Into thine hand I commit my spirit: thou hast redeemed me, O Lord God of truth.

6 I have hated them that regard lying vanities: but I trust in the Lord.

7 I will be glad and rejoice in thy mercy: for thou hast considered my trouble; thou hast known my soul in adversities;

8 And hast not shut me up into the hand of the enemy: thou hast set my feet in a large room.

9 Have mercy upon me, O Lord, for I am in trouble: mine eye is consumed with grief, yea, my soul and my belly.

10 For my life is spent with grief, and my years with sighing: my strength faileth because of mine iniquity, and my bones are consumed.

11 I was a reproach among all mine enemies, but especially among my neighbours, and a fear to mine acquaintance: they that did see me without fled from me.

12 I am forgotten as a dead man out of mind: I am like a broken vessel.

13 For I have heard the slander of many: fear was on every side: while they took counsel together against me, they devised to take away my life.

14 But I trusted in thee, O Lord: I said, Thou art my God.

15 My times are in thy hand: deliver me from the hand of mine enemies, and from them that persecute me.

16 Make thy face to shine upon thy servant: save me for thy mercies' sake.

17 Let me not be ashamed, O Lord; for I have called upon thee: let the wicked be ashamed, and let them be silent in the grave.

18 Let the lying lips be put to silence; which speak grievous things proudly and contemptuously against the righteous.
19 Oh how great is thy goodness, which thou hast laid up for them that fear thee; which thou hast wrought for them that trust in thee before the sons of men!
20 Thou shalt hide them in the secret of thy presence from the pride of man: thou shalt keep them secretly in a pavilion from the strife of tongues.

21 Blessed be the LORD: for he hath shewed me his marvellous kindness in a strong city.
22 For I said in my haste, I am cut off from before thine eyes: nevertheless thou heardest the voice of my supplications when I cried unto thee.
23 O love the LORD, all ye his saints: for the LORD preserveth the faithful, and plentifully rewardeth the proud doer.
24 Be of good courage, and he shall strengthen your heart, all ye that hope in the LORD.

Psalm 31 Clarification

1 In you, O LORD, I put my trust; let me never be ashamed: deliver me in to your righteousness.
2 Hear me, deliver me quickly; be my strong rock in a house of defense to save me.
3 For you are my rock and my fortress; For your name's sake lead me, and guide me.
4 Pull me out of the trap that they secretly laid for me: for you are my strength.

5 Into your hand I commit my spirit: you have redeemed me, O LORD God of truth.
6 I hated them that respect lying idols: but I trust in the LORD.
7 I will be glad and rejoice in your mercy: for you have considered my trouble; you known my soul in misfortune; 8 You have not given me into the hands of the enemy: you have placed me in a spacious place.
9 Have mercy upon me, O LORD, for I am in trouble: my eyes are

consumed with grief, down to my soul and my belly.

10 For my life is consumed with grief, and my years with sighing: my strength fails because of my iniquity, and my bones are weak.

11 I was a disappointment to all my enemies, but especially to my neighbors, and an object of fear to my acquaintance: The ones who saw me on the street fled from me.

12 I am forgotten as though I were dead: I am like a broken vessel.

13 For I have heard the slander of many: fear was on every side: they worked together and plotted to kill me.

14 But I trusted in you, O LORD: I said, you are my God.

15 My life is in your hand: deliver me from the hand of my enemies, and from them that persecute me.

16 Make your face shine on your servant: save me for your mercies' sake.

17 Do not let me be ashamed, O LORD; for I have called on you: let the wicked be ashamed, and let them be silent in the grave.

18 Let the lying lips be silenced; which speak murderous things proudly and hatred against the righteous.

19 Oh how great is your goodness, which you laid up for them that fear you; which you have shaped them that trust in you before the sons of men!

20 You will hide them in your secret presence from the pride of man: you will keep them secretly in a shelter away from the lies.

21 Blessed be the LORD: for he has shown me his marvelous kindness in a strong city.

22 For I said in my haste, I am cut off from before your eyes: nevertheless you still heard my prayer when I cried on to you.

23 O love the LORD, all of you who are his saints: for the LORD preserves the faithful, and pays back the proud.

24 Be of good courage, and he shall strengthen your heart, all of you who placed their hope in the LORD.

Definitions

Privily
Word Definition:
Secret
Contextual Definition:
Secret, concealed, not made known in public
Substitution Word/phrase for clarity:
"Secret"

Adversities
Word Definition:
Ongoing difficulty or misfortune
Contextual Definition:
On going difficulty or misfortune
Substitution Word/phrase for clarity:
"misfortune"

Reproach
Word Definition:
Disapproval or disappointment; Blame
Contextual Definition:
Disapproval or disappointment; Blame
Substitution Word/phrase for clarity:
"disappointment"

Grievous
Word Definition:
To have severe pain; to suffer; to have sorrow
Contextual Definition:
To have severe pain; to suffer; to have sorrow
Substitution Word/phrase for clarity:
"murderous"

Contemptuously
Word Definition:
To show or feel extreme hatred to someone
Contextual Definition:
Scornful, or hatred or disapproval
Substitution Word/phrase for clarity:
"hatred"

Wrought
Word Definition:
Mold or worked into a form in a deliberate way
Contextual Definition:
Mold or worked into a form in a deliberate way
Substitution Word/phrase for clarity:
"shape"

Pavilion
Word Definition:
A decorative building, structure or tent
Contextual Definition:
A shelter or fort
Substitution Word/phrase for clarity:
"Shelter"

Scripture 20
Luke 11:1-13 KJV

¹ And it came to pass, that, as he was praying in a certain place, when he ceased, one of his disciples said unto him, Lord, teach us to pray, as John also taught his disciples.

² And he said unto them, When ye pray, say, Our Father which art in heaven, Hallowed be thy name. Thy kingdom come. Thy will be done, as in heaven, so in earth.

³ Give us day by day our daily bread.

⁴ And forgive us our sins; for we also forgive every one that is indebted to us. And lead us not into temptation; but deliver us from evil.

⁵ And he said unto them, Which of you shall have a friend, and shall go unto him at midnight, and say unto him, Friend, lend me three loaves;

⁶ For a friend of mine in his journey is come to me, and I have nothing to set before him?

⁷ And he from within shall answer and say, Trouble me not: the door is now shut, and my children are with me in bed; I cannot rise and give thee.

⁸ I say unto you, Though he will not rise and give him, because he is his friend, yet because of his importunity he will rise and give him as many as he needeth.

⁹ And I say unto you, Ask, and it shall be given you; seek, and ye shall find; knock, and it shall be opened unto you.

¹⁰ For every one that asketh receiveth; and he that seeketh findeth; and to him that knocketh it shall be opened.

¹¹ If a son shall ask bread of any of you that is a father, will he give him a stone? or if he ask a fish, will he for a fish give him a serpent?

¹² Or if he shall ask an egg, will he offer him a scorpion?

¹³ If ye then, being evil, know how to give good gifts unto your children: how much more shall your heavenly Father give the Holy Spirit to them that ask him?

Luke 11:1-13 Clarification

1 One day, Jesus was praying in a certain place, when he finished, one of his disciples said to him, Lord, teach us to pray, just as John taught his disciples.

2 And he said to them, When you pray, say, "Our Father which are in heaven, Hallowed be your name. Your kingdom come. Your will be done, as in heaven, so in earth.

3 Give us day by day our daily bread.

4 And forgive us our sins; for we also forgive every one that is indebted to us. And lead us not into temptation; but deliver us from evil."

5 And he said to them, "Which of you have a friend, and go to him at midnight, and say to him, "Friend, lend me three loaves; 6 For another friend of mines stopped by, and I do not have any food to give him"

7 And your friend inside answer and say to you, "don't bother: the door is shut, and my children are with me in bed; I cannot get up and give you anything".

8 Now I say to you, though he wouldn't get up and give you any bread just because you are his friend, he will get up and give you as much as you need because of your persistence.

9 And I say to you, Ask, and it will be given to you; seek, and you will find; knock, and it will be opened for you.

10 For every one that asks they will receive; and he that seeks will find; and to him that knocks it will be opened.

11 If a son asks for bread from any of you that is a father, will he give him a stone? or if he asks for a fish, will he give him a serpent?

12 Or if he asks for an egg, will he offer him a scorpion?

13 If you, being evil, know how to give good gifts to your children: how much more shall your heavenly Father give the Holy Spirit to them that ask him?

Definitions

Hallowed
Word Definition:
Sacred; Consecrated
Contextual Definition:
Sacred; Consecrated
Substitution Word/phrase for clarity:
"hallowed"

Importunity
Word Definition:
Requesting in an Annoying or overly persistent way
Contextual Definition:
Persistence, insistence; over-eagerness
Substitution Word/phrase for clarity:
"persistent"

Chapter 3 Activities

Complete the following passages by picking the correct word from the Word List below. Then find the words in the word-search puzzle on the next page.

Word List:
A. Yielding   B. Healed   C. Dead   D. Given   E. Living   F. Blessed
G. Destructions   H. Trust   I. Righteousness   J. Seek
K. Commit   L. Knock   M. Trouble   N. Ourselves   O. Bestowed

1. For none of us liveth to himself, and no man dieth to himself. For whether we live, we live unto the Lord; and whether we die, we die unto the Lord: whether we live therefore, or die, we are the Lord's. For to this end Christ both died, and rose, and revived, that he might be Lord both of the _____ and _____. (Romans 14:7-9 KJV) [Reading: Romans 14:1-13]

2. But we had the sentence of death in ourselves that we should not trust in _____, but in God which raiseth the dead: Who delivered us from so great a death, and doth deliver: in whom we trust that he will yet deliver us; Ye also helping together by prayer for us, that for the gift _____ upon us by the means of many persons thanks may be given by many on our behalf. (2 Corinthians 1:9-11 KJV) [Reading: 2 Corinthians 1:3-11]

3. Heal me, O Lord, and I shall be _____; save me, and I shall be saved: for thou art my praise. Behold, they say unto me, Where is the word of the Lord? let it come now. (Jeremiah 17:14-15 KJV) [Reading: Jeremiah 17:14-18]

4. _____ is the man that _____ in the Lord, and whose hope the Lord is. For he shall be as a tree planted by the waters, and that spreadeth out her roots by the river, and shall not see when heat cometh, but her leaf shall be green; and shall not be careful in the year of drought, neither shall cease from _____ fruit. (Jeremiah 17:7-8 KJV) [Reading: Jeremiah 17:1-13]

5. Then they cry unto the Lord in their _____, and he saveth them out of their distresses. He sent his word, and healed them, and delivered them from their _____. Oh that men would praise the Lord for his goodness, and for his wonderful works to the children of men! (Psalm 107:19-21 KJV) [Reading: Psalm 107]

6. In thee, O Lord, do I put my trust; let me never be ashamed: deliver me in thy _____. Bow down thine ear to me; deliver me speedily: be thou my strong rock, for an house of defence to save me. For thou art my rock and my fortress; therefore for thy name's sake lead me, and guide me. Pull me out of the net that they have laid privily for me: for thou art my strength. Into thine hand I _____ my spirit: thou hast redeemed me, O Lord God of truth. (Psalm 31:1-5 KJV) [Reading: Psalms 31]

7. And I say unto you, Ask, and it shall be _____ you; _____, and ye shall find; _____, and it shall be opened unto you. For every one that asketh receiveth; and he that seeketh findeth; and to him that knocketh it shall be opened. (Luke 11:9-10 KJV) [Reading: Luke 11:1-13]

Find the missing words from the passages on the previous page in the word-search puzzle below.

Word List:

Yielding	Healed	Dead	Given	Living	Blessed
Destructions	Trust	Righteousness	Seek		
Commit	Knock	Trouble	Ourselves	Bestowed	

```
S  U  T  I  O  N  S  R  F  B  Y  E  A  D  R  Q  E  Y
H  E  A  L  W  F  O  U  R  L  E  T  O  B  W  T  W  I
I  B  L  E  S  S  E  D  R  U  E  R  R  E  F  U  G  E
Q  O  S  Y  O  U  B  L  E  F  S  O  O  U  E  T  K  R
H  E  P  S  D  E  S  Y  T  G  E  U  K  Q  S  H  E  A
U  E  U  D  E  A  D  E  T  I  R  B  O  S  U  T  Y  P
W  R  P  Z  Y  N  Z  S  Y  V  N  L  E  S  T  R  U  T
I  C  F  B  T  W  S  Y  G  E  I  E  L  I  V  I  N  G
K  O  T  L  O  E  K  U  X  N  U  Y  S  R  U  E  W  I
L  M  A  E  E  Z  R  T  O  U  R  S  E  L  V  E  S  D
H  M  S  W  V  E  U  C  R  E  X  Y  O  P  E  T  I  E
U  I  P  L  H  Q  K  F  G  H  T  L  R  A  O  R  F  S
R  T  R  A  P  E  X  E  S  D  P  H  X  E  C  U  O  T
Y  P  U  B  L  Y  A  X  O  C  K  I  G  D  K  W  Z  R
I  U  S  R  Q  G  Z  L  U  B  Y  N  Y  I  V  B  I  U
E  S  E  E  K  T  P  Q  E  W  I  I  T  F  R  E  V  C
P  I  X  C  K  A  Y  X  K  D  Z  L  X  A  P  S  I  T
E  T  O  U  R  I  L  E  L  R  G  H  C  F  P  T  N  I
Z  N  G  O  L  I  R  E  P  X  L  I  E  U  Y  O  G  O
K  E  E  W  Q  U  I  N  G  Z  O  X  T  E  L  W  Y  N
I  I  T  B  L  Y  E  S  Y  U  O  U  Q  W  I  E  E  S
Y  C  A  P  E  T  Z  S  S  D  E  A  T  R  G  D  I  S
```

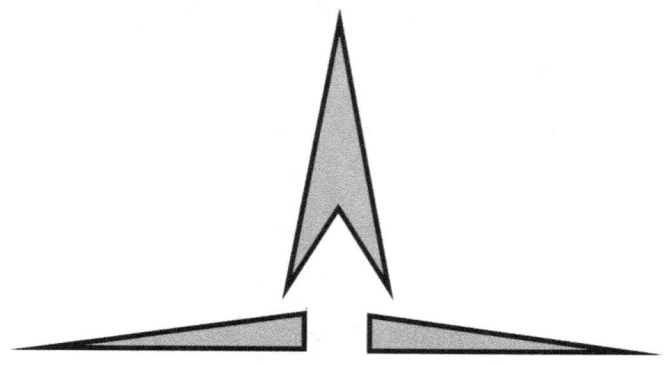

My God, I believe in you. My Lord, I believe in you. I confess that I am not double minded (having both belief and unbelief) when it comes to believing in you. There is no doubt that you are my God and my Creator. There is no doubt that you are my Lord and my Savior. My Lord, you came that I may have life and enjoy the life God gave me. All of your promises to me are answered by a "yes" and "it is done." But I do not love you for what you can do for me, I do not love you for what I can get from you, I love you because you first loved me. I am extremely grateful for your love and for how it has changed my life for the good. Now I can rest in your love and find peace in your love. And for everything that I am and for everything that I have and for everything that I do not have... I will always praise you. Amen.

Chapter 4
Praise Is What I Do

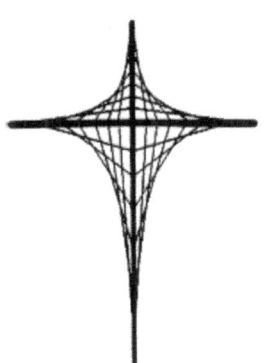

When you accepted Christ, it guaranteed that everything will work out for your good because of the Lord. No matter what you are going through: it will work out in your favor. Always confess with your mouth how you want things to look when you come out of whatever you are facing. Do not be discouraged by the things you can see. Instead, be motivated by them. When things are not going how you intended them to go, use that as fuel to ignite a greater fire within you. Use that fire to confess more, to dream more, to believe more, to praise God more and that will bring you out of whatever you are in. As a believer, the greater the problem you face, the hotter that fire will burn within you, making you determined to make it through.

Never forget that the Lord does not send trouble to teach you, a believer, a lesson. Nor does He create trouble in order to get your attention. Trouble can come to anyone because there is a devil who wants to destroy all of the people on this earth (both Christians and non-Christians). The devil influences mankind in order to put both temporary and lifelong systems in place to cause uncertainty, chaos, division, and jealousy, which ultimately bring trouble to all mankind. This is why trouble can come to anyone, regardless of what they believe. All of this is designed to amplify fear and greed in mankind by making man fear the unknown and crave possessions to make them feel safe. But don't be fooled; not all of our trouble comes from the devil or his systems. We can also face trouble in our lives because of the choices and decisions we have made – whether consciously or subconsciously.

Our trouble will never overtake us because what God does for the believer is absolutely amazing. He will show you His glory, power, mercy, and grace in the midst of your troubles. He will show you his glory by going before you and setting up a way out. He will show you His power by strengthening you to be able to withstand anything that comes your way. He will show you his mercy by hardening the hearts of those who need to be hardened and softening the hearts of the ones who need softening. He will show you His grace by giving you dominion to bring to life things that need to live and to death to things that need to die. Whatever is needed, God will supply. So, fear not, for the Lord your God is with you. He has strengthened you, He has equipped you, and He has given you all the power and dominion you need to overcome anything in this world. You are equipped with these things because of God and not because of anything that you did or didn't do. Since you accepted Jesus into your heart and into your life, you have access to everything that God has equipped you with. So, give God all the praise, for He is good.

Psalms 150 KJV

1 Praise ye the Lord. Praise God in his sanctuary: praise him in the firmament of his power.

2 Praise him for his mighty acts: praise him according to his excellent greatness.

3 Praise him with the sound of the trumpet: praise him with the psaltery and harp.

4 Praise him with the timbrel and dance: praise him with stringed instruments and organs.

5 Praise him upon the loud cymbals: praise him upon the high sounding cymbals.

6 Let every thing that hath breath praise the Lord. Praise ye the Lord.

Psalms 150 Clarification

1 All of you, praise the Lord. Praise God in his sanctuary: praise him in the heavens for his power.

2 Praise him for his mighty acts: praise him according to his excellent greatness.

3 Praise him with the sound of the trumpet: praise him with the psaltery and harp.

4 Praise him with the timbrel and dance: praise him with stringed instruments and organs.

5 Praise him with the loud cymbals: praise him with the high sounding cymbals.

6 Let everything that hath breath praise the Lord. All of you, praise the Lord.

Definitions

Firmament
> Word Definition:
>> Heaven or top of the sky
>
> Contextual Definition:
>> The heavens
>
> Substitution Word/phrase for clarity:
>> "Heavens"

Psaltery
> Word Definition:
>> An ancient musical instrument with a flat soundboard that is played by plucking the strings with the fingers or a plectrum.
>
> Contextual Definition:
>> A musical instrument with a flat soundboard that is played by plucking the strings with the fingers or a plectrum.
>
> Substitution Word/phrase for clarity:
>> "Psaltery"

Timbrel
> Word Definition:
>> A tambourine or an alike instrument
>
> Contextual Definition:
>> A tambourine or an alike instrument
>
> Substitution Word/phrase for clarity:
>> "Timbrel"

Scripture 22
Isaiah 29:17-24 KJV

17 Is it not yet a very little while, and Lebanon shall be turned into a fruitful field, and the fruitful field shall be <u>esteemed</u> as a forest?

18 And in that day shall the deaf hear the words of the book, and the eyes of the blind shall see out of <u>obscurity</u>, and out of darkness.

19 The meek also shall increase their joy in the Lord, and the poor among men shall rejoice in the Holy One of Israel.

20 For the terrible one is brought to nought, and the <u>scorner</u> is consumed, and all that watch for <u>iniquity</u> are cut off:

21 That make a man an <u>offender</u> for a word, and lay a <u>snare</u> for him that <u>reproveth</u> in the gate, and turn aside the just for a thing of nought.

22 Therefore thus saith the Lord, who <u>redeemed</u> Abraham, concerning the house of Jacob, Jacob shall not now be ashamed, neither shall his face now wax pale.

23 But when he seeth his children, the work of mine hands, in the midst of him, they shall sanctify my name, and sanctify the Holy One of Jacob, and shall fear the God of Israel.

24 They also that <u>erred</u> in spirit shall come to understanding, and they that murmured shall learn doctrine.

Isaiah 29:17-24 Clarification

17 In a short amount of time, Lebanon will be turned into a fruitful field, and the fruitful field will be regarded as a forest.

18 In that day the deaf shall hear the words in the book, and the eyes of the blind will see out of their blindness and see out of the darkness.

19 The humble will also increase their joy in the Lord, and the poor will rejoice in the Holy One of Israel.

20 For the terrible one is brought to nothing, the hateful one is consumed, and all who desire wickedness are cut off.

21 Those who are able to make an innocent man guilty by their word,

and lay a trap for him who show compassion in the gate, and falsely accuse the innocent.

22 Therefore so says the Lord, who rescued Abraham, concerning the house of Jacob: "Jacob shall not be ashamed, Nor shall his face turn pale; 23 But when he sees his children, The work of My hands, in his midst, They will sanctify My name, And sanctify the Holy One of Jacob, And fear the God of Israel.

24 Those who also strayed in the spirit will come to understanding, And those who complained will learn doctrine."

Definitions

Esteemed
    Word Definition:
        To be respected or highly valued
    Contextual Definition:
        To be seen as something valuable
    Substitution Word/phrase for clarity:
        "regarded"

Obscurity
    Word Definition:
        Not to see clearly
    Contextual Definition:
        Not to see clearly
    Substitution Word/phrase for clarity:
        "blindness"

Scorner
    Word Definition:
        Openly dislike someone; To angrily disrespect or mock someone
    Contextual Definition:
        To be filled with hate and disrespect
    Substitution Word/phrase for clarity:
        "hateful"

Iniquity
    Word Definition:
        A wicked act or sin
    Contextual Definition:
        Having a desire for wicked acts or things
    Substitution Word/phrase for clarity:
        "desire wickedness"

Offender
    Word Definition:
        To break a law or rule. To sin
    Contextual Definition:
        To be guilty of violating or breaking the law
    Substitution Word/phrase for clarity:
        "guilty"

Snare
    Word Definition:
        A noose or trap made to catch animals
    Contextual Definition:
        To set a trap
    Substitution Word/phrase for clarity:
        "trap"

Reproveth
    Word Definition:
        To censure or gently correct
    Contextual Definition:
        To censure or gently correct
    Substitution Word/phrase for clarity:
        "show compassion"

Redeemed
    Word Definition:
        To be restored from any faults or consequences by a form of payment; Cleared
    Contextual Definition:
        To take back or rescue
    Substitution Word/phrase for clarity:
        "Rescue"

Erred

Word Definition:
To make a mistake or sin
Contextual Definition:
To stray from what is right
Substitution Word/phrase for clarity:
"strayed"

Scripture 23
Luke 18:35-43 KJV

³⁵ And it came to pass, that as he was come <u>nigh</u> unto Jericho, a certain blind man sat by the way side begging: ³⁶ And hearing the multitude pass by, he asked what it meant.

³⁷ And they told him, that Jesus of Nazareth passeth by.

³⁸ And he cried, saying, Jesus, thou son of David, have mercy on me.

³⁹ And they which went before <u>rebuked</u> him, that he should hold his peace: but he cried so much the more, Thou son of David, have mercy on me.

⁴⁰ And Jesus stood, and commanded him to be brought unto him: and when he was come near, he asked him,

⁴¹ Saying, What <u>wilt</u> thou that I shall do unto thee? And he said, Lord, that I may receive my sight.

⁴² And Jesus said unto him, Receive thy sight: thy faith hath saved thee.

⁴³ And immediately he received his sight, and followed him, glorifying God: and all the people, when they saw it, gave praise unto God.

Luke 18:35-43 Clarification

³⁵ And it came to pass, that as he was approaching Jericho, there was a certain blind man sitting on the side begging: ³⁶ And hearing the multitude pass by, he asked what was happening.

³⁷ And they told him, that Jesus of Nazareth is passing by.

³⁸ And he cried out, saying, Jesus, the son of David, have mercy on me.

³⁹ And those that were in front of him tried to quiet him, and told him to hold his peace: then he cried out louder, the son of David, have mercy on me.

⁴⁰ And Jesus stood, and commanded him to be brought to him: and when he was near, Jesus asked him,

⁴¹ Saying, What did you want me to do for you? And he said, Lord, that I may receive my sight.

⁴² And Jesus said unto him, Receive your sight: your faith has saved you.

43 And immediately he received his sight, and followed him, glorifying God: and all the people, when they saw it, gave praise unto God.

Definitions

Nigh

Word Definition:
Near in location, time, or association

Contextual Definition:
Start to approach something or get close to something

Substitution Word/phrase for clarity:
"Approaching"

Rebuked

Word Definition:
Strongly disapprove or criticize

Contextual Definition:
Try to quiet or silence because one's disapproval

Substitution Word/phrase for clarity:
"quiet"

Wilt

Word Definition:
Present tense of Will

Contextual Definition:
Present tense of "will"

Substitution Word/phrase for clarity:
"Will"

Scripture 24
John 12 KJV

1 Then Jesus six days before the passover came to Bethany, where Lazarus was, which had been dead, whom he raised from the dead.

2 There they made him a supper; and Martha served: but Lazarus was one of them that sat at the table with him.

3 Then took Mary a pound of ointment of spikenard, very costly, and anointed the feet of Jesus, and wiped his feet with her hair: and the house was filled with the odour of the ointment.

4 Then saith one of his disciples, Judas Iscariot, Simon's son, which should betray him, 5 Why was not this ointment sold for three hundred pence, and given to the poor?

6 This he said, not that he cared for the poor; but because he was a thief, and had the bag, and bare what was put therein.

7 Then said Jesus, Let her alone: against the day of my burying hath she kept this.

8 For the poor always ye have with you; but me ye have not always.

9 Much people of the Jews therefore knew that he was there: and they came not for Jesus' sake only, but that they might see Lazarus also, whom he had raised from the dead.

10 But the chief priests consulted that they might put Lazarus also to death; 11 Because that by reason of him many of the Jews went away, and believed on Jesus.

12 On the next day much people that were come to the feast, when they heard that Jesus was coming to Jerusalem, 13 Took branches of palm trees, and went forth to meet him, and cried, Hosanna: Blessed is the King of Israel that cometh in the name of the Lord.

14 And Jesus, when he had found a young ass, sat thereon; as it is written, 15 Fear not, daughter of Sion: behold, thy King cometh, sitting on an ass's colt.

16 These things understood not his disciples at the first: but when Jesus was glorified, then remembered they that these things were written of

him, and that they had done these things unto him.

17 The people therefore that was with him when he called Lazarus out of his grave, and raised him from the dead, bare record.

18 For this cause the people also met him, for that they heard that he had done this miracle.

19 The Pharisees therefore said among themselves, Perceive ye how ye prevail nothing? behold, the world is gone after him.

20 And there were certain Greeks among them that came up to worship at the feast: 21 The same came therefore to Philip, which was of Bethsaida of Galilee, and desired him, saying, Sir, we would see Jesus.

22 Philip cometh and telleth Andrew: and again Andrew and Philip tell Jesus.

23 And Jesus answered them, saying, The hour is come, that the Son of man should be glorified.

24 Verily, verily, I say unto you, Except a corn of wheat fall into the ground and die, it abideth alone: but if it die, it bringeth forth much fruit.

25 He that loveth his life shall lose it; and he that hateth his life in this world shall keep it unto life eternal.

26 If any man serve me, let him follow me; and where I am, there shall also my servant be: if any man serve me, him will my Father honour.

27 Now is my soul troubled; and what shall I say? Father, save me from this hour: but for this cause came I unto this hour.

28 Father, glorify thy name. Then came there a voice from heaven, saying, I have both glorified it, and will glorify it again.

29 The people therefore, that stood by, and heard it, said that it thundered: others said, An angel spake to him.

30 Jesus answered and said, This voice came not because of me, but for your sakes.

31 Now is the judgment of this world: now shall the prince of this world be cast out.

32 And I, if I be lifted up from the earth, will draw all men unto me.

33 This he said, signifying what death he should die.

34 The people answered him, We have heard out of the law that Christ

abideth for ever: and how sayest thou, The Son of man must be lifted up? who is this Son of man?

³⁵ Then Jesus said unto them, Yet a little while is the light with you. Walk while ye have the light, lest darkness come upon you: for he that walketh in darkness knoweth not whither he goeth.

³⁶ While ye have light, believe in the light, that ye may be the children of light. These things spake Jesus, and departed, and did hide himself from them.

³⁷ But though he had done so many miracles before them, yet they believed not on him: ³⁸ That the saying of Esaias the prophet might be fulfilled, which he spake, Lord, who hath believed our report? and to whom hath the arm of the Lord been revealed?

³⁹ Therefore they could not believe, because that Esaias said again,

⁴⁰ He hath blinded their eyes, and hardened their heart; that they should not see with their eyes, nor understand with their heart, and be converted, and I should heal them.

⁴¹ These things said Esaias, when he saw his glory, and spake of him.

⁴² Nevertheless among the chief rulers also many believed on him; but because of the Pharisees they did not confess him, lest they should be put out of the synagogue: ⁴³ For they loved the praise of men more than the praise of God.

⁴⁴ Jesus cried and said, He that believeth on me, believeth not on me, but on him that sent me.

⁴⁵ And he that seeth me seeth him that sent me.

⁴⁶ I am come a light into the world, that whosoever believeth on me should not abide in darkness.

⁴⁷ And if any man hear my words, and believe not, I judge him not: for I came not to judge the world, but to save the world.

⁴⁸ He that rejecteth me, and receiveth not my words, hath one that judgeth him: the word that I have spoken, the same shall judge him in the last day.

⁴⁹ For I have not spoken of myself; but the Father which sent me, he

gave me a commandment, what I should say, and what I should speak. [50] And I know that his commandment is life everlasting: whatsoever I speak therefore, even as the Father said unto me, so I speak.

John 12 Clarification

[1] Six days before the passover, Jesus came to Bethany where Lazarus, whom he raised from the dead, was.

[2] There they made him supper and Martha served: Lazarus was one of them that sat at the table with him.

[3] Then Mary took a pound of a very costly ointment called spikenard, and anointed the feet of Jesus and wiped his feet with her hair: and the house was filled with the scent from the ointment.

[4] Then one of his disciples, Judas Iscariot, Simon's son, which will betray him, [5] asked Why wasn't the expensive ointment sold for three hundred pence and given to the poor?

[6] He said this not because he cared for the poor but because he was a thief and held the money bag and helped himself to what was in it.

[7] Then Jesus said, Leave her alone: she kept this for the day of my burying.

[8] You will always have the poor with you; but you will not always have me.

[9] Many of the Jews knew that Jesus was there: But they didn't come just to see Jesus, they also came to see Lazarus, who was raised from the dead.

[10] But the chief priest consulted that they might put Lazarus to death as well; [11] Because of Lazarus, many of the Jews turned away from them and believed on Jesus.

[12] The next day many people came to the feast, when they heard that Jesus was coming to Jerusalem, [13] They took branches of palm trees, and went forth to meet him, and cried Hosanna: Blessed is the King of Israel that cometh in the name of the Lord.

14 Then Jesus found a young donkey and sat on it to fulfill what was written.

15 For it was written: Fear not, daughter of Sion: behold, thy King cometh, sitting on a donkey's colt.

16 His disciples did not understand what was happening at first: but when Jesus was glorified, they remembered that these things were written about him, and is being fulfilled

17 The people who were with Jesus when he called Lazarus out of his grave, raising him from the grave, bare witness.

18 For this reason the people also met him, for they heard of this miracle.

19 The Pharisees said among themselves, Can you see? Are we accomplishing anything? Look, the world is still following him.

20 There were certain Greeks among them that came to worship at the feast: 21 One of the Greeks that came was Philip of Bethsaida of Galilee, and said: Sir, we want to see Jesus.

22 Philip came and told Andrew: and Andrew and Philip told Jesus.

23 And Jesus answered them saying, The hour is come, that the Son of man should be glorified.

24 In truth, I say unto you, if a corn of wheat falls into the ground and doesn't die, it remains alone: but if the corn of wheat dies, it will bring forth much fruit.

25 One that loves their soul in the worldly system will be destroying it; and they that hate their soul in the worldly system will guard it until they enter into eternal life.

26 If any man serve me, let him follow me; and where I am, he will be there with me: if any man serve me, my Father will honor them.

27 Now my soul is troubled; and what shall I say? Father, save me from this hour: but I am here for this hour.

28 Father, glorify thy name. Then came a voice from heaven saying, I have both glorified it and will glorify it again.

29 The people who stood by, heard it, and said that it thundered: Others said that an angel spoke to him.

30 Jesus answered and said, This voice came not for my sake but for yours.

31 Now is the judgment of this world: now shall the prince of this world be cast out.

32 And for me, if I am lifted up from the earth, I will draw all unto me.

33 This is what Jesus said, signifying how he should die.

34 Then the people answered him saying, We have heard out of the law that Christ will live and be with us forever: Why do you say, The Son of man must be lifted up? Who is this Son of man?

35 Then Jesus said unto them, Yet a little while is the light with you. Walk while you have the light, unless the darkness will fall on you: for he that walks in darkness does not know where they are going.

36 While you have the light, believe in the light, that you may be the children of the light. These are the things that Jesus spoke, and then he departed, and did not hide himself from them.

37 But though he had done so many miracles before them, they still did not believe in him: 38 This is as the prophet Esaias prophesied that is being fulfilled. He said, Lord, who hath believed our report? And to whom has the arm of the Lord been revealed?

39 Therefore they could not believe, because that Esaias said again, 40 He blinded their eyes, and hardened their heart; that they should not see with their eyes, nor understand with their heart, and be converted, and I should heal them.

41 Esaias said these things when he saw his glory and spoke of him

42 Nevertheless, among all of the chief rulers, many believed in him; but because of the Pharisees, they did not confess him out of fear of being kicked out of the synagogue:

43 For they loved the praise of men more than the praise of God.

44 Jesus cried out and said, whoever that believes in me, doesn't believe in me, but believes in the one who sent me.

45 And whoever sees me, has seen the one who sent me.

46 I have come as the light into the world, that whosoever believes in me should not I've in darkness.

47 and if anyone hears my words, and does not believe, I will not judge him: Because I did not come to

judge the world, instead, I came to save the world.

⁴⁸ Whoever rejects me, and does not believe my words, will have one who will judge him: the word that I have spoken, will be the same word that will judge them in the last day.

⁴⁹ I do not speak for myself, I speak for the Father who sent me, he gave me the commandment on what I should say and what I should speak. ⁵⁰ And I know that his commandment is life everlasting: whatsoever I speak, I am following what the Father spoke to me to say to you.

Definitions

Spikenard
Word Definition:
A aromatic Himalayan plant, Nardostachys Jatamansi, of the Valerian family
Contextual Definition:
Aromatic substance made from an Indian plant that was used as a perfume in ancient times
Substitution Word/phrase for clarity:
"Spikenard"

Pence
Word Definition:
Penny (plural)
Contextual Definition:
A set number of pennies
Substitution Word/phrase for clarity:
"Pence"

Perceive
Word Definition:
To realize something through ones senses
Contextual Definition:
Use your senses to become aware of something
Substitution Word/phrase for clarity:
"see"

Prevail
Word Definition:
To overcome by one's strength, effectiveness, or superiority
Contextual Definition:
To overcome by one's strength, effectiveness, or superiority
Substitution Word/phrase for clarity:
"accomplishing"

Behold
Word Definition:
To see or observe or watch
Contextual Definition:
To perceive through sight
Substitution Word/phrase for clarity:
"Look"

Verily
Word Definition:
To speak confidently in truth
Contextual Definition:
Confidently speak in truth
Substitution Word/phrase for clarity:
"in truth"

Abideth
Word Definition:
To tolerate or endure
Contextual Definition:
To remain or to live; not to die
Substitution Word/phrase for clarity:
"live"/"remain"/"be with"

Scripture 25
Ephesians 1 KJV

¹ Paul, an apostle of Jesus Christ by the will of God, to the saints which are at Ephesus, and to the faithful in Christ Jesus: ² Grace be to you, and peace, from God our Father, and from the Lord Jesus Christ.

³ Blessed be the God and Father of our Lord Jesus Christ, who hath blessed us with all spiritual blessings in heavenly places in Christ:

⁴ According as he hath chosen us in him before the foundation of the world, that we should be holy and without blame before him in love:

⁵ Having predestinated us unto the adoption of children by Jesus Christ to himself, according to the good pleasure of his will,

⁶ To the praise of the glory of his grace, wherein he hath made us accepted in the beloved.

⁷ In whom we have redemption through his blood, the forgiveness of sins, according to the riches of his grace;

⁸ Wherein he hath abounded toward us in all wisdom and prudence;

⁹ Having made known unto us the mystery of his will, according to his good pleasure which he hath purposed in himself:

¹⁰ That in the dispensation of the fulness of times he might gather together in one all things in Christ, both which are in heaven, and which are on earth; even in him:

¹¹ In whom also we have obtained an inheritance, being predestinated according to the purpose of him who worketh all things after the counsel of his own will:

¹² That we should be to the praise of his glory, who first trusted in Christ.

¹³ In whom ye also trusted, after that ye heard the word of truth, the gospel of your salvation: in whom also after that ye believed, ye were sealed with that holy Spirit of promise,

¹⁴ Which is the earnest of our inheritance until the redemption of the purchased possession, unto the praise of his glory.

15 Wherefore I also, after I heard of your faith in the Lord Jesus, and love unto all the saints,

16 Cease not to give thanks for you, making mention of you in my prayers;

17 That the God of our Lord Jesus Christ, the Father of glory, may give unto you the spirit of wisdom and revelation in the knowledge of him:

18 The eyes of your understanding being enlightened; that ye may know what is the hope of his calling, and what the riches of the glory of his inheritance in the saints,

19 And what is the exceeding greatness of his power to us-ward who believe, according to the working of his mighty power,

20 Which he wrought in Christ, when he raised him from the dead, and set him at his own right hand in the heavenly places,

21 Far above all principality, and power, and might, and dominion, and every name that is named, not only in this world, but also in that which is to come:

22 And hath put all things under his feet, and gave him to be the head over all things to the church,

23 Which is his body, the fulness of him that filleth all in all.

Ephesians 1 Clarification

1 Paul, an apostle of Jesus Christ by the will of God, to the saints which are at Ephesus, and to the faithful in Christ Jesus: 2 Grace be to you, and peace, from God our Father, and from the Lord Jesus Christ.

3 Blessed be the God and Father of our Lord Jesus Christ, who hath blessed us with all spiritual blessings in heavenly places in Christ: 4 Before the foundation of the world, he chose us to be in him, and that we should be holy and without blame before him in love:

5 Having already arranged for us to be the adopted children by Jesus Christ unto himself, according to the good pleasure of his will, 6 Praise be to the glory of his grace, his grace that allowed us to be accepted in the beloved.

7 In him we have our redemption through his blood, the forgiveness of sins, all according to the riches of

his grace; **8** Where he have greatly supplied us in all wisdom and discretion; **9** Having made known to us the mystery of his will, according to his good pleasure which he already attained in himself: **10** Distributing the fullness of times in a way that he might come together as one in Christ, both which are in heaven, and which are on earth; even in him: **11** In whom we have obtained an inheritance, arranged according to the purpose of him who work all things after the counsel of his own will: **12** That we should represent the praise of his glory, who first trusted in Christ. **13** In whom you also trusted, and after trusting, you heard the word of truth, which is the gospel of your salvation: in whom you believed, you were sealed with that holy Spirit of promise, **14** Which is an important part of our inheritance until the redemption of the purchased possession, unto the praise of his glory.

15 Where I also, after I heard of your faith in the Lord Jesus, and love to all the saints, **16** I do not stop giving thanks for you, mentioning you in my prayers; **17** That the God of our Lord Jesus Christ, the Father of glory, may give unto you the spirit of wisdom and revelation in the knowledge of him: **18** The eyes of your understanding being enlightened; that you may know what the hope of his calling is, and the riches of the glory of his inheritance in the saints, **19** And what is the exceeding greatness of his power towards us who believe, according to the working of his mighty power, **20** Which he shaped us in Christ, when he raised him from the dead, and set him at his own right hand in the heavenly places, **21** Far above all principality, and power, and might, and dominion, and every name that is named, not only in this world, but also in that which is to come: **22** And has placed all things under his feet, and gave him to be the head over all things to the church, **23** Which is his body, the fullness of him that fills all in all.

Definitions

Predestinated
Word Definition:
Determined ahead of time by higher power; fate
Contextual Definition:
Arrange a plan in advance
Substitution Word/phrase for clarity:
"Already arranged"

Abounded
Word Definition:
Large in number or amount; to be plentiful
Contextual Definition:
To give generously and abundantly
Substitution Word/phrase for clarity:
"supplied"

Prudence
Word Definition:
To have discipline or use reason
Contextual Definition:
To have discipline or use reason
Substitution Word/phrase for clarity:
"discretion"

Dispensation
Word Definition:
A system of order. Something dispensed
Contextual Definition:
To deal out something
Substitution Word/phrase for clarity:
"Distributing"

Earnest
Word Definition:
Serious; Important; Great
Contextual Definition:
Serious; Important; Great
Substitution Word/phrase for clarity:
"Important"

Wrought
Word Definition:
Molded or worked into a form in a deliberate way
Contextual Definition:
Brought into some form
Substitution Word/phrase for clarity:
"shaped"

Scripture 26
1 Peter 2 KJV

¹ Wherefore laying aside all <u>malice</u>, and all <u>guile</u>, and hypocrisies, and envies, and all evil speakings, ² As newborn babes, desire the sincere milk of the word, that ye may grow thereby: ³ If so be ye have tasted that the Lord is gracious.

⁴ To whom coming, as unto a living stone, <u>disallowed</u> indeed of men, but chosen of God, and precious, ⁵ Ye also, as lively stones, are built up a spiritual house, an holy priesthood, to offer up spiritual sacrifices, acceptable to God by Jesus Christ.

⁶ Wherefore also it is contained in the scripture, Behold, I lay in Sion a chief corner stone, elect, precious: and he that believeth on him shall not be <u>confounded</u>.

⁷ Unto you therefore which believe he is precious: but unto them which be disobedient, the stone which the builders disallowed, the same is made the head of the corner, ⁸ And a stone of stumbling, and a rock of offence, even to them which stumble at the word, being disobedient: whereunto also they were appointed.

⁹ But ye are a chosen generation, a royal priesthood, an holy nation, a peculiar people; that ye should shew <u>forth</u> the praises of him who hath called you out of darkness into his marvellous light; ¹⁰ Which in time past were not a people, but are now the people of God: which had not obtained mercy, but now have obtained mercy.

¹¹ Dearly beloved, I <u>beseech</u> you as strangers and pilgrims, abstain from fleshly lusts, which war against the soul; ¹² Having your conversation honest among the Gentiles: that, whereas they speak against you as evildoers, they may by your good works, which they shall behold, glorify God in the day of visitation.

¹³ Submit yourselves to every <u>ordinance</u> of man for the Lord's sake: whether it be to the king, as supreme; ¹⁴ Or unto governors, as unto them that are sent by him for the punishment of evildoers, and for the praise of them that do well.

15 For so is the will of God, that with well doing ye may put to silence the ignorance of foolish men: 16 As free, and not using your liberty for a cloke of maliciousness, but as the servants of God.

17 Honour all men. Love the brotherhood. Fear God. Honour the king.

18 Servants, be subject to your masters with all fear; not only to the good and gentle, but also to the froward.

19 For this is thankworthy, if a man for conscience toward God endure grief, suffering wrongfully.

20 For what glory is it, if, when ye be buffeted for your faults, ye shall take it patiently? but if, when ye do well, and suffer for it, ye take it patiently, this is acceptable with God.

21 For even hereunto were ye called: because Christ also suffered for us, leaving us an example, that ye should follow his steps: 22 Who did no sin, neither was guile found in his mouth: 23 Who, when he was reviled, reviled not again; when he suffered, he threatened not; but committed himself to him that judgeth righteously: 24 Who his own self bare our sins in his own body on the tree, that we, being dead to sins, should live unto righteousness: by whose stripes ye were healed.

25 For ye were as sheep going astray; but are now returned unto the Shepherd and Bishop of your souls.

1 Peter 2 Clarification

1 Therefore laying aside all spite, and all cunning, and hypocrisies, and envies, and all evil speaking,

2 As newborn babes, you desire the sincere milk of the word, that you may grow from it: 3 because you have tasted that the Lord is gracious.

4 To those who come to the living stone, rejected by men, but chosen by God, and precious, 5 You, as lively stones, built a spiritual house, a holy priesthood, to offer up spiritual sacrifices, acceptable to God by Jesus Christ.

6 Therefore it is also contained in the scripture: Behold, I lay in Zion a chief corner stone, elect, precious: and he that believeth on him shall not be damned.

7 To you who believe that they are precious: remember those who are disobedient, the stone that the builders rejected, they are made the head of the corner, 8 And a stone of stumbling, and a rock of offence, even to them which stumble at the word, being disobedient: remember that they were appointed.

9 But you are a chosen generation, a royal priesthood, an holy nation, a peculiar people; that you should show in plain view the praises of him who called you out of the darkness and into his marvelous light; 10 Which were not a people in the past, but are now the people of God: which had not obtained mercy in the past, but now have obtained mercy.

11 Dearly beloved, I beg you as strangers and pilgrims, abstain from fleshly lusts, which is in war against the soul; 12 Have an honest conversation with the Gentiles: even though they speak against you as evildoers, so that they may glorify God in the day of visitation by your good works which they shall behold.

13 Submit yourselves to every decree of man for the Lord's sake: whether it be to the king, as supreme; 14 Or unto governors, as unto them that are sent by him for the punishment of evildoers, and for the praise of them that do well.

15 For this is also the will of God, that with well-doing you may put to silence the ignorance of foolish men: 16 being free, and not using your liberty as a covering for hatefulness, but using your liberty as servants of God.

17 Honor all men. Love the brotherhood. Fear God. Honor the king.

18 Servants, be subject to your masters with all fear; not only to the good and gentle, but also to the difficult.

19 For this by grace, if a man through the conscience of God endure grief, suffering wrongfully.

20 For what glory it is, if, when you are struck for your faults, you shall take it patiently? but if, when you do well, and suffer for it, you take it patiently, this is acceptable with God.

21 For even to this you were called: because Christ also suffered for us, leaving us an example, that you

should follow in his footsteps: 22 Who did not sin, neither was guile found in his mouth: 23 Who, when he was insulted, he did not insult back; when he suffered, he did not threaten them; but committed himself to him that judge righteously: 24 Who alone carried our sins within his own body on the tree, that we, being dead to sins, should live unto righteousness: by whose stripes were healed by.

25 For you were as sheep going astray; but have now returned to the Shepherd and Bishop of your souls.

Definitions

Malice

    Word Definition:
        Wanting to cause pain, harm; to trouble someone or something

    Contextual Definition:
        Wanting to cause pain, harm; to intentionally trouble someone

    Substitution Word/phrase for clarity:
        "spite"

Guile

    Word Definition:
        Deceitful, sneaky, or cunning

    Contextual Definition:
        Deceitful, sneaky, or cunning

    Substitution Word/phrase for clarity:
        "cunning"

Disallowed

    Word Definition:
        To deny any validity of someone or something

    Contextual Definition:
        To refuse to allow

    Substitution Word/phrase for clarity:
        "Rejected"

Confounded

    Word Definition:
        Confused, perplexed, annoyance

    Contextual Definition:
        To be damned or cursed or condemned

    Substitution Word/phrase for clarity:
        "damned"

Forth

    Word Definition:
        To notice or bring into view

    Contextual Definition:
        To bring into view

    Substitution Word/phrase for clarity:
        "In plain view"

Beseech

    Word Definition:
        To beg or to urgently ask someone to do something

    Contextual Definition:
        To beg

    Substitution Word/phrase for clarity:
        "Beg"

Ordinance

    Word Definition:
        A decree, command or order

    Contextual Definition:
        A decree, command or order

    Substitution Word/phrase for clarity:
        "decree"

Cloke

    Word Definition:
        A Cloak; A cape or loose garment

    Contextual Definition:
        A covering

    Substitution Word/phrase for clarity:
        "covering"

Maliciousness
Word Definition:
A desire to cause harm to someone
Contextual Definition:
A desire to cause harm to someone
Substitution Word/phrase for clarity:
"hatefulness"

Servants
Word Definition:
One that carries out tasks for a master or employer
Contextual Definition:
Man or woman who carries out tasks for a master or lord
Substitution Word/phrase for clarity:
"servant"

Froward
Word Definition:
To be difficult or disobedient or in opposition
Contextual Definition:
Perverse, disobedient; peevish, petulant; adverse, difficult
Substitution Word/phrase for clarity:
"difficult"

Buffeted
Word Definition:
A blow
Contextual Definition:
To strike with a fist or open hand
Substitution Word/phrase for clarity:
"Strike"

Reviled
Word Definition:
Verbal abuse
Contextual Definition:
Verbal abuse
Substitution Word/phrase for clarity:
"Insulted"

<u>Scripture 27</u>
1 Peter 4:1-11 KJV

¹ Forasmuch then as Christ hath suffered for us in the flesh, <u>arm</u> yourselves likewise with the same mind: for he that hath suffered in the flesh hath ceased from sin; ² That he no longer should live the rest of his time in the flesh to the lusts of men, but to the will of God. ³ For the time past of our life may suffice us to have <u>wrought</u> the will of the Gentiles, when we walked in <u>lasciviousness</u>, lusts, excess of wine, <u>revellings</u>, <u>banquetings</u>, and <u>abominable</u> idolatries: ⁴ Wherein they think it strange that ye run not with them to the same excess of <u>riot</u>, speaking evil of you: ⁵ Who shall give account to him that is ready to judge the <u>quick</u> and the dead. ⁶ For for this cause was the gospel preached also to them that are dead, that they might be judged according to men in the flesh, but live according to God in the spirit. ⁷ But the end of all things is at hand: be ye therefore sober, and watch unto prayer. ⁸ And above all things have <u>fervent charity</u> among yourselves: for charity shall cover the multitude of sins. ⁹ Use hospitality one to another without grudging. ¹⁰ As every man hath received the gift, even so minister the same one to another, as good stewards of the <u>manifold</u> grace of God. ¹¹ If any man speak, let him speak as the oracles of God; if any man minister, let him do it as of the ability which God giveth: that God in all things may be glorified through Jesus Christ, to whom be praise and dominion for ever and ever. Amen.

1 Peter 4:1-11 Clarification

¹ Since Christ suffered in the flesh for us, therefore, strengthen yourselves like Christ with the same mindset: those that suffer in the flesh are done with sin; ² And no longer live the rest of their lives in the flesh for the lusts of men, but live for the will of God. ³ For our past may have satisfied us by changing for the will of the

Gentiles, as we walked in lasciviousness, lusts, excess of wine, revellings, banquetings, and abominable idolatries: ⁴ Now they find it strange that you no longer run with them to the same level as before – without control or restraint, and now, they speak evil of you:

⁵ Who shall give account to him that is ready to judge the living and the dead.

⁶ For this is the reason why the gospel is preached to them that are dead, so that they might be judged according to men in the flesh, but live according to God in the spirit.

⁷ But the end of all things is at hand: be sober and watch, and be in prayer.

⁸ And above all things have passionate love among yourselves: for love will cover the multitude of sins.

⁹ Be hospitable to each other without being resentful.

¹⁰ As every man received a gift, minister the same to one another, as good stewards of the manifold grace of God.

¹¹ If any man speak, let him speak as the oracles of God; if any man minister, let him do it to the ability that God gave him: that God in all things may be glorified through Jesus Christ, to whom be praise and dominion for ever and ever. Amen.

Definitions

Arm
Word Definition:
  Power; Strength
Contextual Definition:
  Power; Strength
Substitution Word/phrase for clarity:
  "strengthen"

Wrought
Word Definition:
  Molded or worked into a form in a deliberate way
Contextual Definition:
  Brought into some form
Substitution Word/phrase for clarity:
  "change"

Lasciviousness
Word Definition:
  Sexual desire; lust
Contextual Definition:
  To be excessive in sensual pleasures of any kind
Substitution Word/phrase for clarity:
  "lasciviousness"

Revellings
Word Definition:
  To take extreme pleasure or satisfaction
Contextual Definition:
  To take extreme pleasure or satisfaction
Substitution Word/phrase for clarity:
  "revellings"

Banquetings
Word Definition:
  To partake in a banquet
Contextual Definition:
  Wild parties
Substitution Word/phrase for clarity:
  "banquetings"

Abominable
Word Definition:
  Disgust or hatred; Detestable
Contextual Definition:
  Abominable
Substitution Word/phrase for clarity:
  "Abominable"

Riot
Word Definition:
  Violent or noisy crowd or group
Contextual Definition:
  Act or move without control or restraint
Substitution Word/phrase for clarity:
  "without control or restraint"

Quick
Word Definition:
  Fast; Alive
Contextual Definition:
  Living, alive, animate, characterized by the presence of life
Substitution Word/phrase for clarity:
  "living"

Fervent

Word Definition:
  Intense feeling; Passionate
Contextual Definition:
  Very hot; Burning;
  Passionate
Substitution Word/phrase for clarity:
  "passionate"

Charity

Word Definition:
  To donate or show kindness
  towards others in need
Contextual Definition:
  To love
Substitution Word/phrase for clarity:
  "love"

Manifold

Word Definition:
  Many; Numerous; A large
  undefined number
Contextual Definition:
  Many; Numerous; A large
  undefined number
Substitution Word/phrase for clarity:
  "manifolc"

Chapter 4 Activities

Complete the following passages by picking the correct word from the Word List below. Then find the words in the word-search puzzle on the next page.

Word List:

A. Chosen B. Immediately C. Firmament D. Predestinated E. Synagogue F. Redemption
G. Instruments H. Meek I. Followed J. Praise K. Greatness L. Darkness M. Through
N. Receive O. Cried P. Stewards Q. Obscurity R. Pharisees S. Forgiveness

1. Praise ye the Lord. _____ God in his sanctuary: praise him in the _____ of his power. Praise him for his mighty acts: praise him according to his excellent _____. Praise him with the sound of the trumpet: praise him with the psaltery and harp. Praise him with the timbrel and dance: praise him with stringed _____ and organs. Praise him upon the loud cymbals: praise him upon the high sounding cymbals. Let everything that hath breath praise the Lord. Praise ye the Lord. (Psalm 150 KJV) [Reading: Psalm 150]

2. And in that day shall the deaf hear the words of the book, and the eyes of the blind shall see out of _____, and out of _____. The _____ also shall increase their joy in the Lord, and the poor among men shall rejoice in the Holy One of Israel. (Isaiah 29:18-19 KJV) [Reading: Isaiah 29:18-20]

3. And Jesus said unto him, _____ thy sight: thy faith hath saved thee. And _____ he received his sight, and _____ him, glorifying God: and all the people, when they saw it, gave praise unto God. (Luke 18:42-43 KJV) [Reading: Luke 18:42-43]

4. Nevertheless among the chief rulers also many believed on him; but because of the _____ they did not confess him, lest they should be put out of the _____: For they loved the praise of men more than the praise of God. Jesus _____ and said, He that believeth on me, believeth not on me, but on him that sent me. (John 12:42-44 KJV) [Reading: John 12]

5. Having _____ us unto the adoption of children by Jesus Christ to himself, according to the good pleasure of his will, To the praise of the glory of his grace, wherein he hath made us accepted in the beloved. In whom we have _____ through his blood, the _____ of sins, according to the riches of his grace; (Ephesians 1:5-7 KJV) [Reading: Ephesians 1]

6. And a stone of stumbling, and a rock of offence, even to them which stumble at the word, being disobedient: where unto also they were appointed. But ye are a _____ generation, a royal priesthood, an holy nation, a peculiar people; that ye should shew forth the praises of him who hath called you out of darkness into his marvelous light; Which in time past were not a people, but are now the people of God: which had not obtained mercy, but now have obtained mercy. (1 Peter 2:8-10 KJV) [Reading: 1 Peter 2]

7. As every man hath received the gift, even so minister the same one to another, as good _____ of the manifold grace of God. If any man speak, let him speak as the oracles of God; if any man minister, let him do it as of the ability which God giveth: that God in all things may be glorified _____ Jesus Christ, to whom be praise and dominion for ever and ever. Amen. (1 Peter 4:10-11 KJV) [Reading: 1 Peter 4:1-12]

Find the missing words from the passages on the previous page in the word-search puzzle below.

Word List:

Chosen   Immediately   Firmament   Predestinated   Synagogue   Redemption

Instruments   Meek   Followed   Praise   Greatness   Darkness   Through

Receive   Cried   Stewards   Obscurity   Pharisees   Forgiveness

```
C  W  H  F  P  Y  P  H  A  R  I  S  E  E  S  X  G  Z  A  X
Q  H  F  O  R  G  I  V  E  N  E  S  S  D  Z  L  Y  G  T  G
Y  B  O  W  O  E  Q  S  S  E  N  O  I  T  P  M  E  D  E  R
X  G  L  S  B  H  D  U  M  B  L  E  X  J  C  J  M  P  W  E
D  R  L  A  E  T  X  E  P  I  E  S  E  D  B  S  J  E  H  V
E  A  O  Z  T  N  E  M  A  M  R  I  F  C  O  R  B  B  A  E
S  T  W  D  C  Z  A  G  H  M  C  E  B  H  B  E  P  O  V  T
B  E  E  V  E  R  W  T  O  J  W  N  C  V  U  D  V  B  E  A
C  R  D  C  P  G  U  G  E  X  V  H  V  E  X  E  G  S  R  H
R  O  B  X  T  H  R  O  U  G  H  N  S  N  I  M  V  C  V  W
I  Y  E  M  E  D  R  C  P  V  D  E  S  A  X  V  B  U  J  B
E  U  G  O  G  A  N  Y  S  B  D  G  C  B  E  B  E  R  N  X
D  L  R  X  Z  U  X  U  H  T  G  N  E  R  T  S  J  I  N  L
S  L  O  B  I  M  M  E  D  I  A  T  E  L  Y  T  R  T  L  U
W  O  D  B  P  Z  X  M  K  R  X  V  Z  B  G  N  L  Y  I  E
H  I  M  E  Q  R  U  S  I  D  D  C  H  O  J  E  I  A  V  P
A  U  R  I  T  Y  K  F  T  E  J  G  A  B  Z  M  U  V  R  C
H  D  N  X  D  A  S  S  W  E  U  H  K  S  M  U  G  L  I  I
G  Y  G  A  I  E  N  L  V  G  W  Y  N  E  A  R  Z  L  D  A
S  R  R  X  D  A  L  I  N  N  V  A  D  T  I  T  E  O  A  R
X  U  E  N  O  U  Y  T  E  U  S  R  Q  S  S  A  W  R  T
Z  C  T  A  F  G  S  K  B  S  C  U  A  D  I  N  E  F  K  E
S  A  U  S  T  I  N  A  T  E  E  E  K  A  S  I  R  I  N  L
C  P  G  J  G  N  R  Y  N  P  R  D  R  Y  C  E  G  J  E  Y
Z  H  D  R  P  H  E  M  S  G  Z  P  E  G  Z  S  W  K  S  B
X  P  O  D  E  U  D  S  M  U  G  O  G  R  S  K  B  A  S  B
H  M  E  E  K  E  F  O  S  A  L  L  X  Z  P  Q  G  O  R  X
```

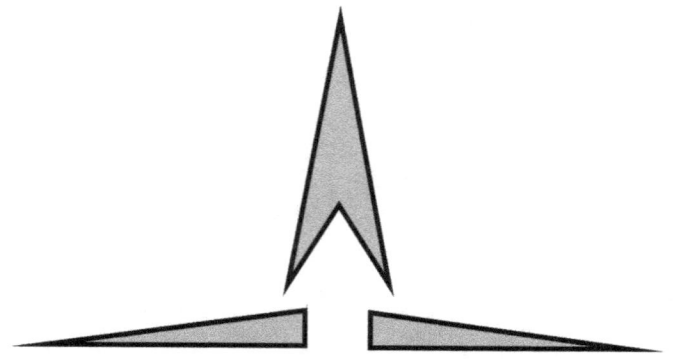

My Lord, I do not deserve all the blessings, love, mercy, and grace you have already given to me, nor the promises that you have for me in the future. But I receive them freely. I receive all that you have for me. Through your blood, you saved me, sanctified me, and delivered me from a world of darkness. You washed away all of my sin forever, you healed my body, you saved my soul. Nothing that I can do will ever come close to earning a single gift that you have freely given to me. I thank you that nothing I do will ever cause me to lose your gifts. For you are great, you are my Lord and Savior, you are the King of Kings and the Lord of Lords. There is none before you and none after you. My God, you are a mighty God, and no one compares to you. You are the God and you are the Lord of my life and I will worship you and give you all the praise and all the glory. For where I am, and what I have, is all because of you. I thank you my Lord; I thank you my God; I thank you my King. Amen.

Chapter 5

I believe in Jesus, I believe in God (Reprise)

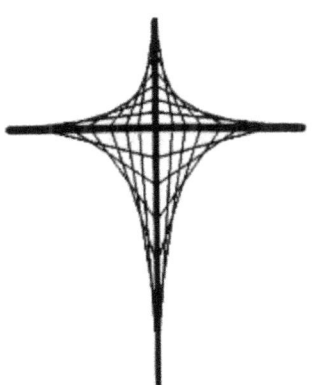

Activities

Fill in the empty grid with the correct answers to the clues listed below. Each answer in the grid consist of one or more words. Use one letter per square.

Clues List:

Across

1 One of Jesus' disciples who walked on water.
4 What type of man did Jesus marvel at because of his great faith that he hasn't seen in all of Israel?
6 The 5th book of the Torah/Pentateuch/Law found in the holy bible.

Down

1 He is the author of the book of Romans.
2 Centurions were members of this group.
3 The mountain that the Lord gave to the children of Israel to take.
5 Who did it please when Jesus was bruised?

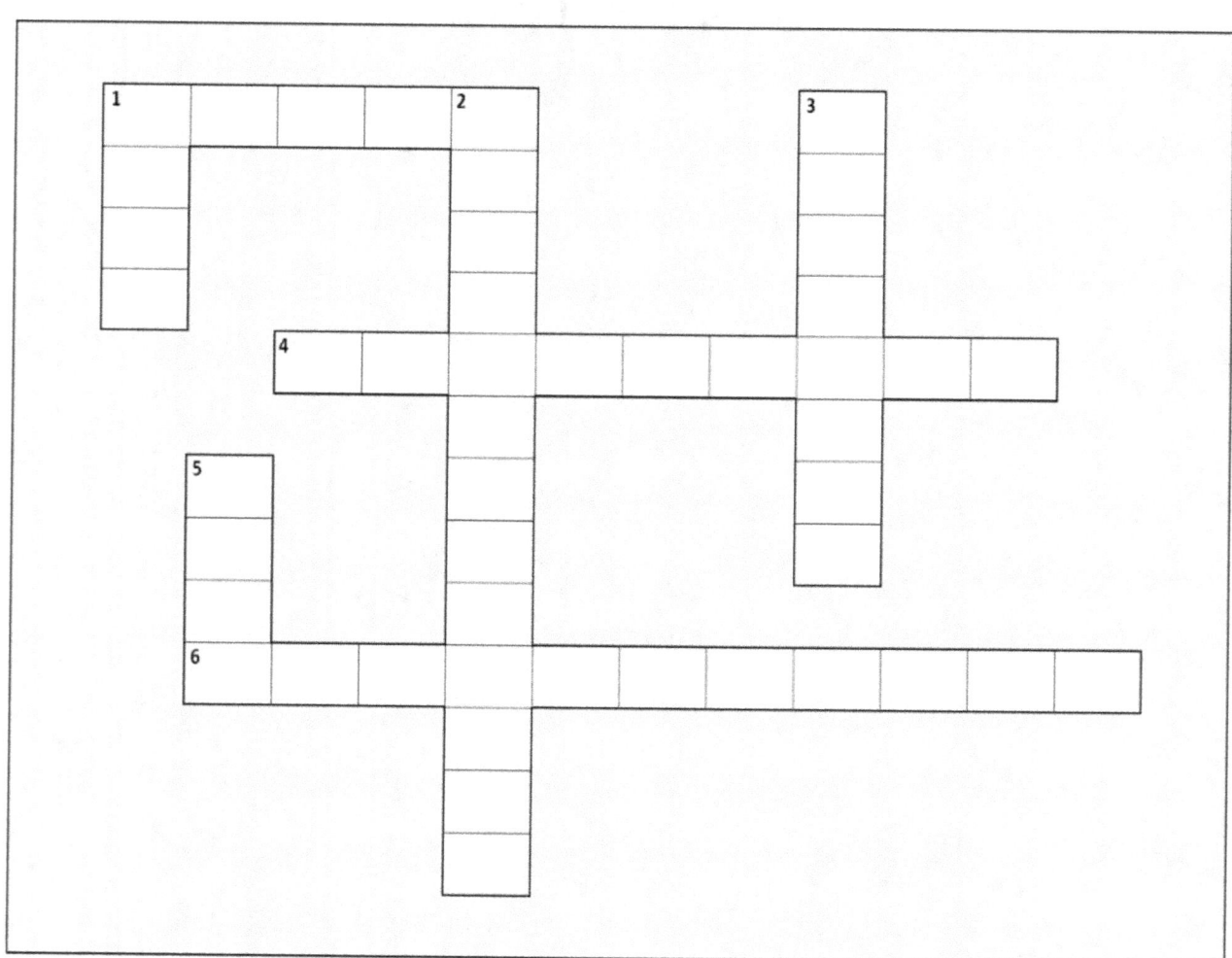

Chapter 6
Not what I deserved, but what I deserve (Reprise)

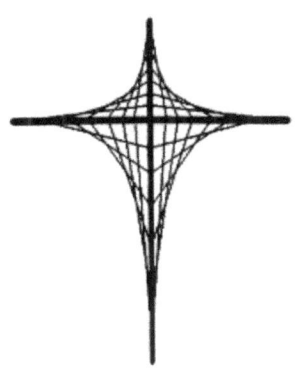

Activities

Fill in the empty grid with the correct answers to the clues listed below. Each answer in the grid consist of one or more words. Use one letter per square.

Clues List:

Across

3 Who visited John to give him revelations on what is to come?

6 His Hebrew name means "God has Hidden" and the Author of the one of the books in the old testaments with less than 5 chapters.

7 Who confronted Peter in Antioch?

8 The Father gave Jesus, the good shepherd, the authority to lay down and take up his _____?

Down

1 What sea did Jesus walk by when he saw two brothers casting a net into the sea?

2 Ephesus, Smyrna, Pergamos, Thyatira, Sardis, Philadelphia, and Laodicea represents what in Asia?

4 Who was the Author of Psalms 103?

5 Who did Peter fear in Antioch that caused him to distance himself from the Gentiles?

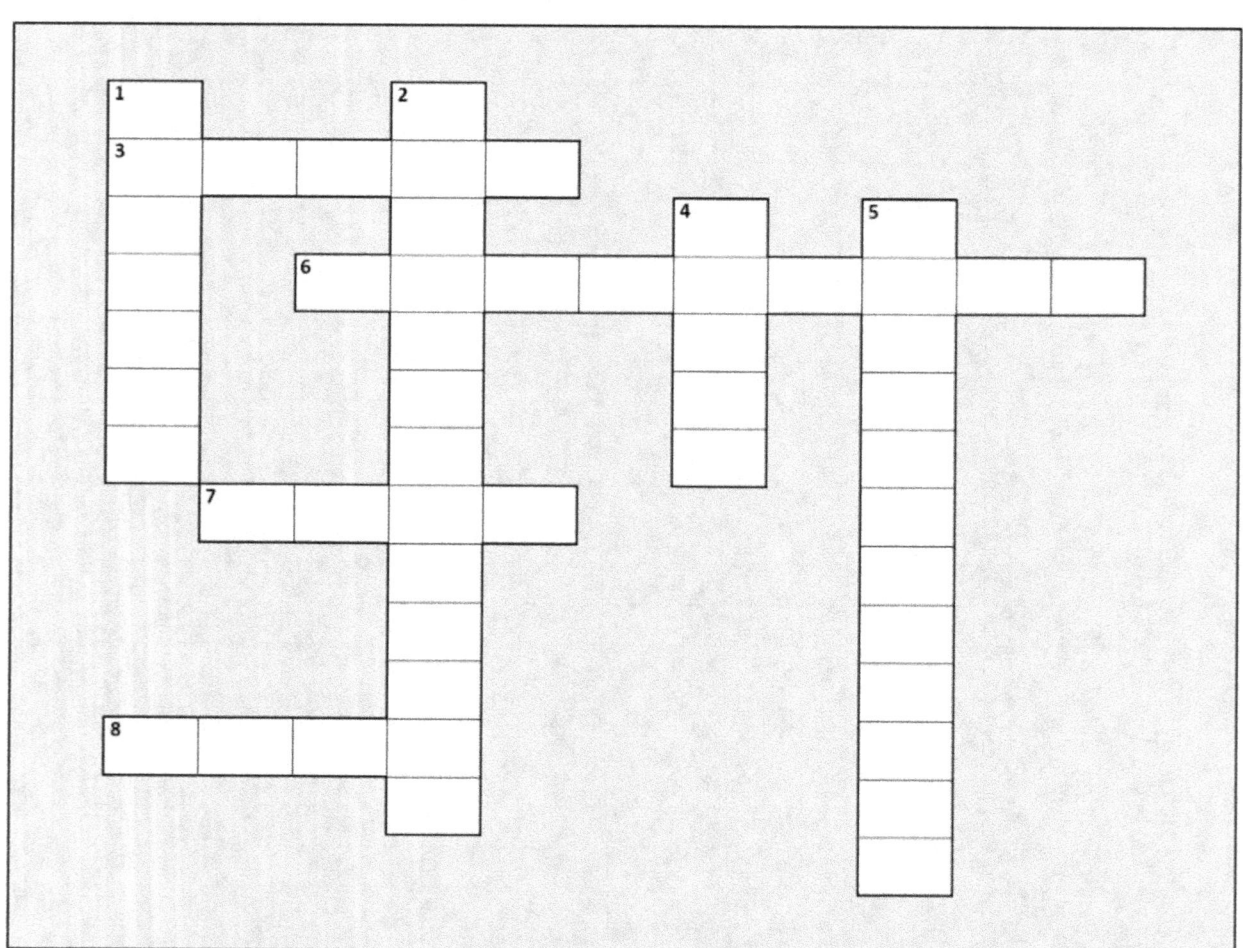

Chapter 7
Be encouraged (Reprise)

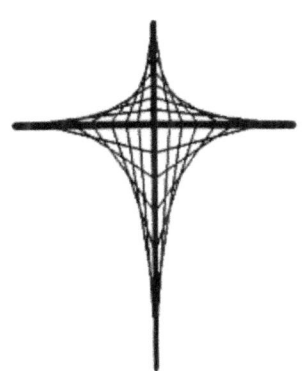

Activities

Fill in the empty grid with the correct answers to the clues listed below. Each answer in the grid consist of one or more words. Use one letter per square.

Clues List:

Across

1 The sins of _____ was written with iron on their hearts and their alters.

5 Paul's letters to the church at Corinth are found in this book.

Down

2 What does God search and test, even if it means giving the person according to their ways and actions?

3 Jesus was asked by his disciples to teach them how to pray because this person taught his disciples.

4 What book of the bible has the most chapters?

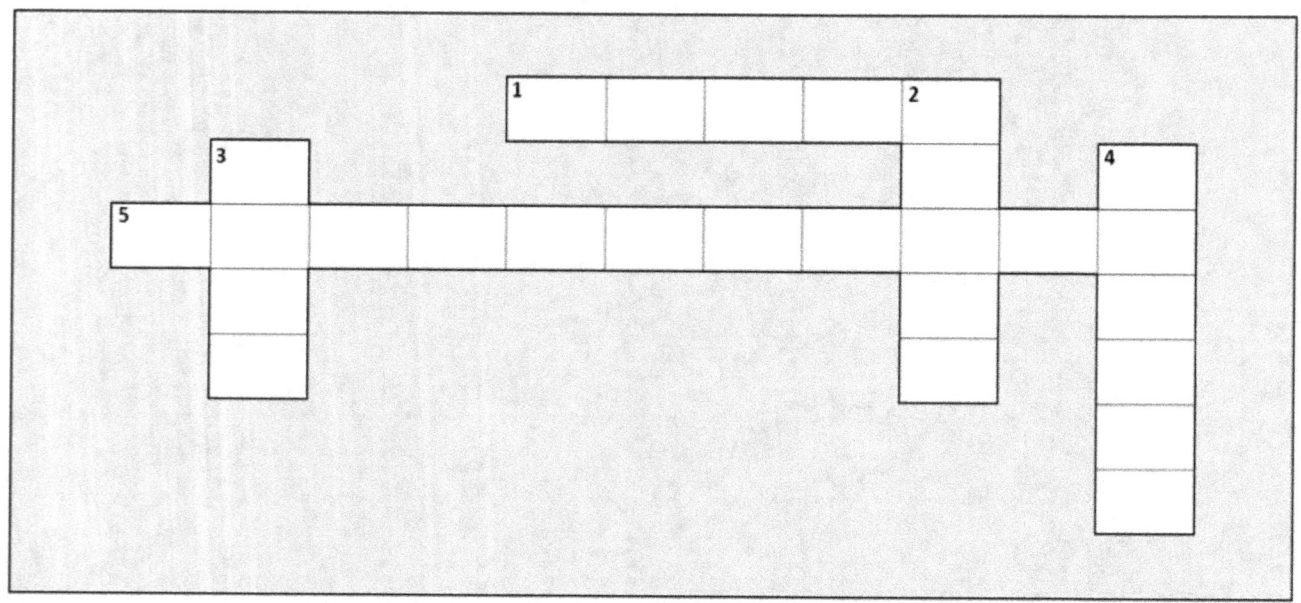

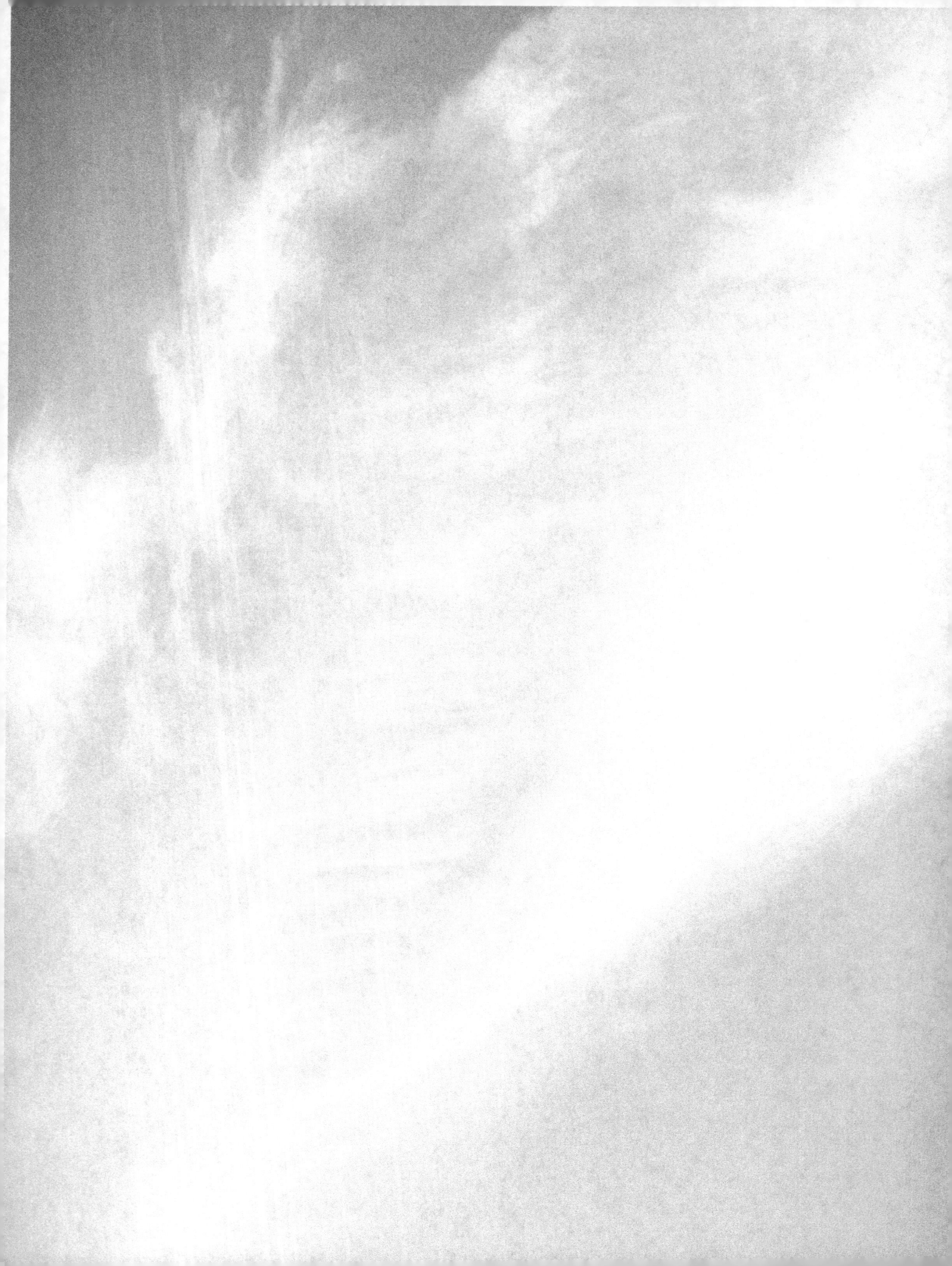

Chapter 8
Praise is what I do (Reprise)

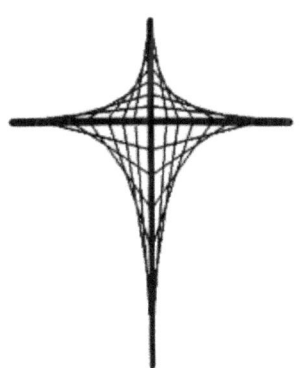

Activities

Fill in the empty grid with the correct answers to the clues listed below. Each answer in the grid consist of one or more words. Use one letter per square.

Clues List:

Across

2 Who was Jesus' and his disciples' treasurer?

4 What was the last name of Simon's son, that was a disciple and who would betray Jesus?

5 Jesus was a Galilean from this place.

6 Before the Passover, the Jews came to Bethany to see Jesus and this man.

Down

1 Jesus was also referred to as the son of this man.

2 The place where Jesus fulfilled the prophecy: "behold thy King cometh, sitting on an ass's colt."

3 Word that is often used to conclude a prayer or end of a letter.

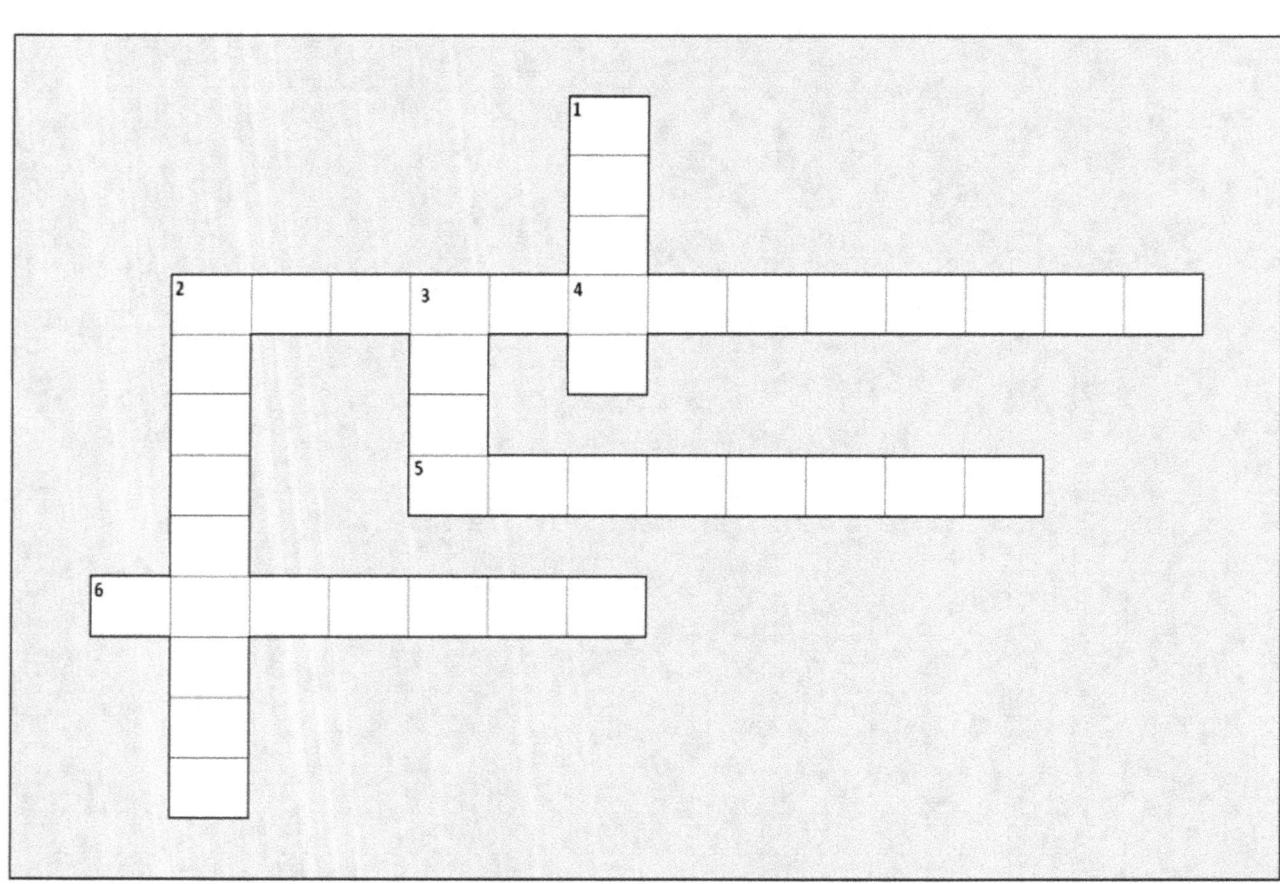

Appendix

Answer Key

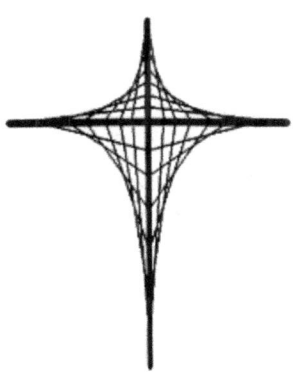

Chapter 1 Fill-in-the-Blank Answers: I believe in Jesus, I believe in God

Complete the following passages by picking the correct word from the Word List below. Then find the words in the word-search puzzle on the next page.

Word List:
A. Stripes   B. Content   C. Immediately   D. Wilderness   E. Faith   F. Believe
G. Healed   H. Wounded   I. Good   J. Jesus   K. Christ   L. Strengthen

1. And we know that all things work together for ____**(I) Good**____ to them that love God, to them who are the called according to his purpose. (Romans 8:28 KJV) [Reading: Romans 8:18-30]

2. But He was ____**(H) Wounded**____ for our transgressions, He was bruised for our iniquities; The chastisement for our peace was upon Him, and by His ____**(A) Stripes**____ we are healed. (Isaiah 53:5 KJV) [Reading: Isaiah 53]

3. O love the Lord, all ye his saints: for the Lord preserveth the faithful, and plentifully rewardeth the proud doer. Be of good courage, and he shall ____**(L) Strengthen**____ your heart, all ye that hope in the Lord. (Psalm 31:23-24 KJV) [Reading: Psalm 31]

4. And in the ____**(D) Wilderness**____, where thou hast seen how that the Lord thy God bare thee, as a man doth bear his son, in all the way that ye went, until ye came into this place. Yet in this thing ye did not ____**(F) Believe**____ the Lord your God, Who went in the way before you, to search you out a place to pitch your tents in, in fire by night, to shew you by what way ye should go, and in a cloud by day. (Deuteronomy 1:31-33 KJV) [Reading: Deuteronomy 1:19-33]

5. And ____**(J) Jesus**____ said unto the centurion, Go thy way; and as thou hast believed, so be it done unto thee. And his servant was ____**(G) Healed**____ in the selfsame hour. (Matthew 8:13 KJV) [Matthew 8:5-13]

6. And **(C) Immediately** Jesus stretched out His hand and caught him, and said to him, "O you of little ____**(E) Faith**____ why did you doubt?" And when they got into the boat, the wind ceased. (Matthew 14:31-32 KJV) [Matthew 14:22-33]

7. Not that I speak in respect of want: for I have learned, in whatsoever state I am, therewith to be ____**(B) Content**____. I know both how to be abased, and I know how to abound: everywhere and in all things I am instructed both to be full and to be hungry, both to abound and to suffer need. I can do all things through ____**(K) Christ**____ which strengtheneth me. (Philippians 4:11-13 KJV) [Reading: Philippians 4:10-20]

Chapter 1 Word-Search Puzzle Answers: I believe in Jesus, I believe in God

Find the missing words from the passages on the previous page in the word-search puzzle below.

Word List:
A. Stripes   B. Content   C. Immediately   D. Wilderness   E. Faith   F. Believe
G. Healed   H. Wounded   I. Jesus   J. Christ   K. Strengthen   L. Good

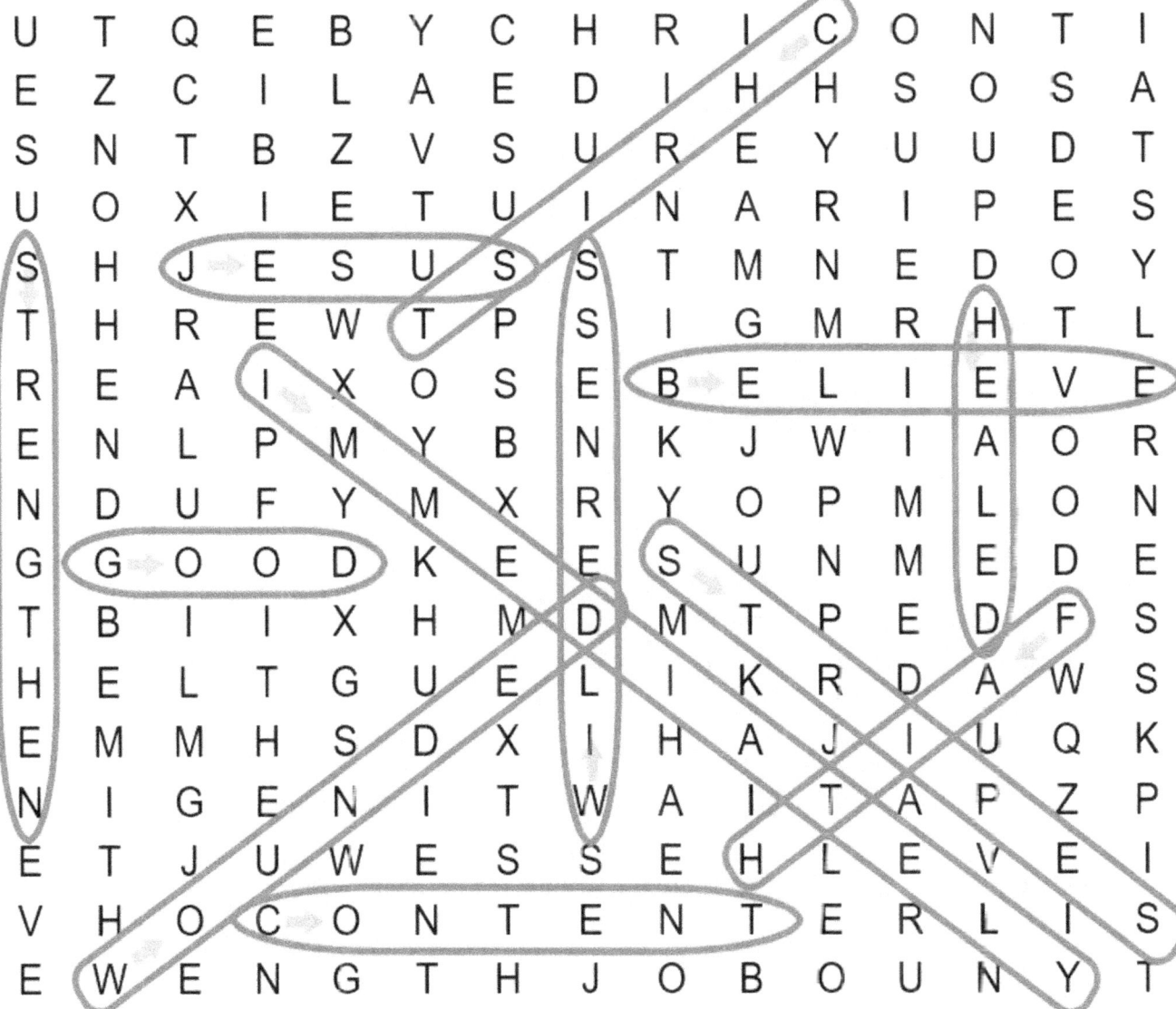

Chapter 2 Fill-in-the-Blank Answers: Not what I deserved, but what I deserve

Complete the following passages by picking the correct word from the Word List below. Then find the words in the word-search puzzle on the next page.

Word List:

A. Abundantly   B. Mighty   C. Rejoice   D. Righteousness   E. Reconciled   F. Transgressions

G. Become   H. Blood   I. Door   J. West   K. Faithful   L. Faith   M. Christ

1. The Lord thy God in the midst of thee is __**(B) Mighty**__; he will save, he will __**(C) Rejoice**__ over thee with joy; he will rest in his love, he will joy over thee with singing (Zephaniah 3:17 KJV) [Reading: Zephaniah 3:9-20]

2. Therefore if any man be in Christ, he is a new creature: old things are passed away; behold, all things are __**(G) Become**__ new (2 Corinthians 5:17 KJV) [Reading: 2 Corinthians 5:1-21]

3. And from Jesus Christ, who is the __**(K) Faithful**__ witness, and the first begotten of the dead, and the prince of the kings of the earth. Unto him that loved us, and washed us from our sins in his own __**(H) Blood**__. (Revelation 1:5 KJV) [Reading: Revelation 1:1-20]

4. Now then we are ambassadors for __**(M) Christ**__, as though God did beseech you by us: we pray you in Christ's stead, be ye __**(E) Reconciled**__ to God (2 Corinthians 5:20 KJV) [Reading: 2 Corinthians 5:1-21]

5. I am crucified with Christ: nevertheless I live; yet not I, but Christ liveth in me: and the life which I now live in the flesh I live by the __**(L) Faith**__ of the Son of God, who loved me, and gave himself for me. I do not frustrate the grace of God: for if __**(D) Righteousness**__ come by the law, then Christ is dead in vain (Galatians 2:20-21 KJV) [Reading: Galatians 2:11-21]

6. As far as the East is from the __**(J) West**__, so far hath he removed our __**(F) Transgressions**__ from us (Psalm 103:12 KJV) [Reading: Psalm 103]

7. I am the __**(I) Door**__: by me if any man enter in, he shall be saved, and shall go in and out, and find pasture. The thief cometh not, but for to steal, and to kill, and to destroy: I am come that they might have life, and that they might have it more __**(A) Abundantly**__. (John 10:9-10 KJV) [Reading: John 10:7-21]

Chapter 2 Word-Search Puzzle Answers: Not what I deserved, but what I deserve

Find the missing words from the passages in the word-search puzzle below.

Word List:

Abundantly Mighty Rejoice Righteousness Reconciled Transgressions

Become Blood Door Faithful Faith Christ West

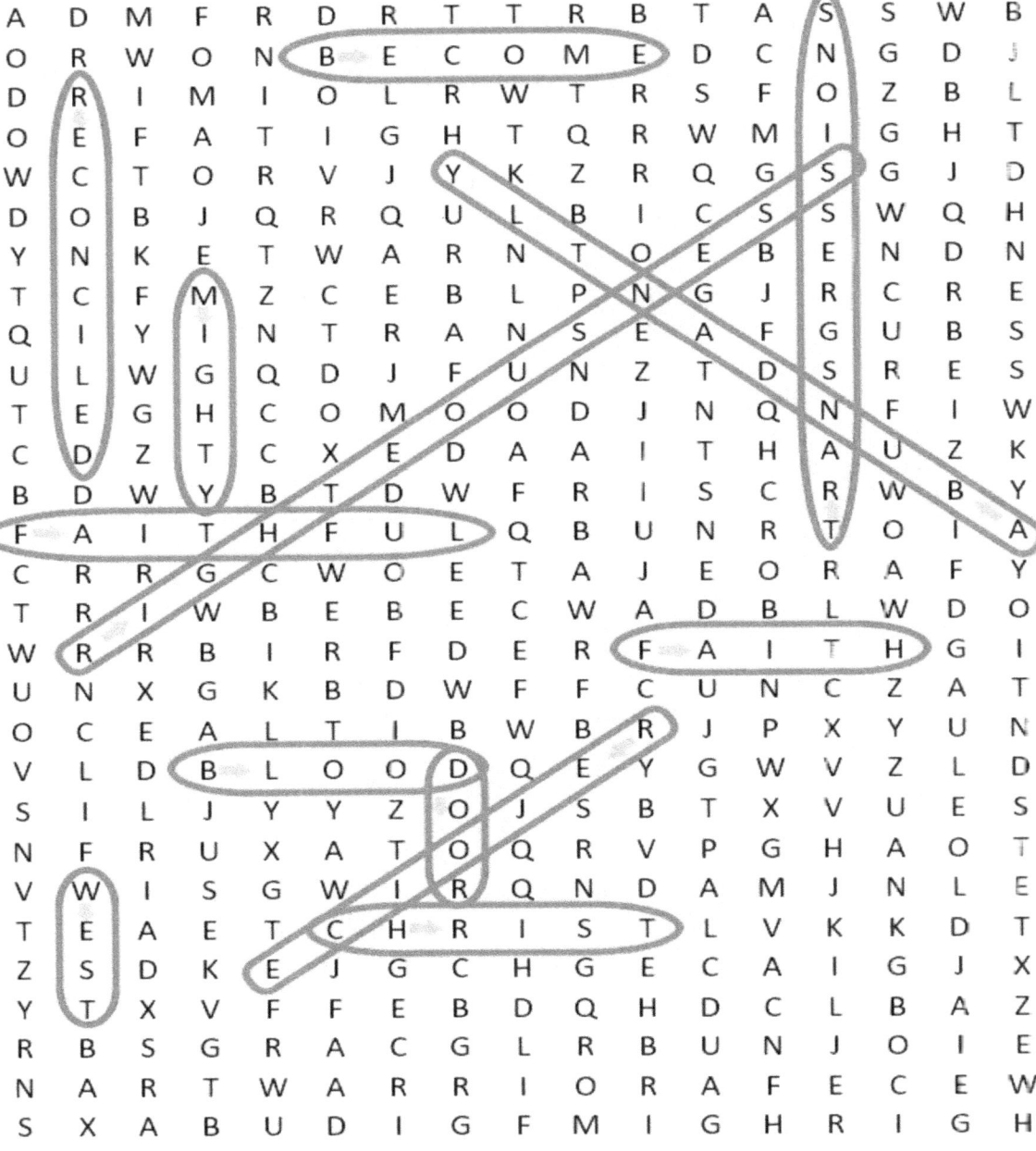

Chapter 3 Fill-in-the-Blank Answers: Be Encouraged

Complete the following passages by picking the correct word from the Word List below. Then find the words in the word-search puzzle on the next page.

Word List:
A. Yielding   B. Healed   C. Dead   D. Given   E. Living   F. Blessed
G. Destructions   H. Trust   I. Righteousness   J. Seek
K. Commit   L. Knock   M. Trouble   N. Ourselves   O. Bestowed

1. For none of us liveth to himself, and no man dieth to himself. For whether we live, we live unto the Lord; and whether we die, we die unto the Lord: whether we live therefore, or die, we are the Lord's. For to this end Christ both died, and rose, and revived, that he might be Lord both of the ___**(E) Living**___ and ___**(C) Dead**___. (Romans 14:7-9 KJV) [Reading: Romans 14:1-13]

2. But we had the sentence of death in ourselves that we should not trust in ___**(N) Ourselves**___, but in God which raiseth the dead: Who delivered us from so great a death, and doth deliver: in whom we trust that he will yet deliver us; Ye also helping together by prayer for us, that for the gift ___**(O) Bestowed**___ upon us by the means of many persons thanks may be given by many on our behalf. (2 Corinthians 1:9-11 KJV) [Reading: 2 Corinthians 1:3-11]

3. Heal me, O Lord, and I shall be ___**(B) Healed**___; save me, and I shall be saved: for thou art my praise. Behold, they say unto me, Where is the word of the Lord? let it come now. (Jeremiah 17:14-15 KJV) [Reading: Jeremiah 17:14-18]

4. ___**(F) Blessed**___ is the man that ___**(H) Trust**___ in the Lord, and whose hope the Lord is. For he shall be as a tree planted by the waters, and that spreadeth out her roots by the river, and shall not see when heat cometh, but her leaf shall be green; and shall not be careful in the year of drought, neither shall cease from ___**(A) Yielding**___ fruit. (Jeremiah 17:7-8 KJV) [Reading: Jeremiah 17:1-13]

5. Then they cry unto the Lord in their ___**(M) Trouble**___, and he saveth them out of their distresses. He sent his word, and healed them, and delivered them from their ___**(G) Destructions**___. Oh that men would praise the Lord for his goodness, and for his wonderful works to the children of men! (Psalm 107:19-21 KJV) [Reading: Psalm 107]

6. In thee, O Lord, do I put my trust; let me never be ashamed: deliver me in thy ___**(I) Righteousness**___. Bow down thine ear to me; deliver me speedily: be thou my strong rock, for an house of defence to save me. For thou art my rock and my fortress; therefore for thy name's sake lead me, and guide me. Pull me out of the net that they have laid privily for me: for thou art my strength. Into thine hand I ___**(K) Commit**___ my spirit: thou hast redeemed me, O Lord God of truth. (Psalm 31:1-5 KJV) [Reading: Psalms 31]

7. And I say unto you, Ask, and it shall be ___**(D) Given**___ you; ___**(J) Seek**___, and ye shall find; ___**(L) Knock**___, and it shall be opened unto you. For every one that asketh receiveth; and he that seeketh findeth; and to him that knocketh it shall be opened. (Luke 11:9-10 KJV) [Reading: Luke 11:1-13]

Chapter 3 Word-Search Puzzle Answers: Be Encouraged

Find the missing words from the passages on the previous page in the word-search puzzle below.

Word List:

Yielding	Healed	Dead	Given	Living	Blessed
Destructions	Trust		Righteousness	Seek	
Commit	Knock	Trouble		Ourselves	Bestowed

```
S  U  T  I  O  N  S  R  F  B  Y  E  A  D  R  Q  E  Y
H  E  A  I  W  F  O  U  R  L  E  T  O  B  W  T  W  I
I  B  L  E  S  S  E  D  R  U  E  R  R  E  F  U  G  E
Q  O  S  Y  O  U  B  L  E  F  S  O  O  U  E  T  K  R
H  E  P  S  D  E  S  Y  T  G  E  U  K  Q  S  H  E  A
U  E  U  D  E  A  D  E  T  I  R  B  O  S  U  T  Y  P
W  R  P  Z  Y  N  Z  S  Y  V  N  L  E  S  T  R  U  T
I  C  F  B  T  W  S  Y  G  E  I  E  L  I  V  I  N  G
K  O  T  L  O  E  K  U  X  N  U  Y  S  R  U  E  W  I
L  M  A  E  E  Z  R  T  O  U  R  S  E  L  V  E  S  D
H  M  S  W  V  E  U  C  R  E  X  Y  O  P  E  T  I  E
U  I  P  L  H  Q  K  F  G  H  T  L  R  A  O  R  F  S
R  T  R  A  P  E  X  E  S  D  P  H  X  E  C  U  O  T
Y  P  U  B  L  Y  A  X  O  C  K  I  G  D  K  W  Z  R
I  U  S  R  Q  G  Z  L  U  B  Y  N  Y  I  V  B  I  U
E  S  E  E  K  T  P  Q  E  W  I  I  T  F  R  E  V  C
P  I  X  C  K  A  Y  X  K  D  Z  L  X  A  P  S  I  T
E  T  O  U  R  I  L  E  L  R  G  H  C  F  P  T  N  I
Z  N  G  O  L  I  R  E  P  X  L  I  E  U  Y  O  G  O
K  E  E  W  Q  U  I  N  G  Z  O  X  T  E  L  W  Y  N
I  I  T  B  L  Y  E  S  Y  U  O  U  Q  W  I  E  E  S
Y  C  A  P  E  T  Z  S  S  D  E  A  T  R  G  D  I  S
```

Chapter 4 Fill-in-the-Blank Answers: Praise is what I do

Complete the following passages by picking the correct word from the Word List below. Then find the words in the word-search puzzle on the next page.

Word List:
A. Chosen B. Immediately C. Firmament D. Predestinated E. Synagogue F. Redemption
G. Instruments H. Meek I. Followed J. Praise K. Greatness L. Darkness M. Through
N. Receive O. Cried P. Stewards Q. Obscurity R. Pharisees S. Forgiveness

1. Praise ye the Lord. _____(J) Praise_____ God in his sanctuary: praise him in the __(C) Firmament__ of his power. Praise him for his mighty acts: praise him according to his excellent __(K) Greatness__. Praise him with the sound of the trumpet: praise him with the psaltery and harp. Praise him with the timbrel and dance: praise him with stringed __(G) Instruments__ and organs. Praise him upon the loud cymbals: praise him upon the high sounding cymbals. Let everything that hath breath praise the Lord. Praise ye the Lord. (Psalm 150 KJV) [Reading: Psalm 150]

2. And in that day shall the deaf hear the words of the book, and the eyes of the blind shall see out of __(Q) Obscurity__, and out of __(L) Darkness__. The _____(H) Meek_____ also shall increase their joy in the Lord, and the poor among men shall rejoice in the Holy One of Israel. (Isaiah 29:18-19 KJV) [Reading: Isaiah 29:18-20]

3. And Jesus said unto him, _____(N) Receive_____ thy sight: thy faith hath saved thee. And __(B) Immediately__ he received his sight, and ____(I) Followed____ him, glorifying God: and all the people, when they saw it, gave praise unto God. (Luke 18:42-43 KJV) [Reading: Luke 18:42-43]

4. Nevertheless among the chief rulers also many believed on him; but because of the __(R) Pharisees__ they did not confess him, lest they should be put out of the ____(E) Synagogue____ : For they loved the praise of men more than the praise of God. Jesus _____(O) Cried_____ and said, He that believeth on me, believeth not on me, but on him that sent me. (John 12:42-44 KJV) [Reading: John 12]

5. Having __(D) Predestinated__ us unto the adoption of children by Jesus Christ to himself, according to the good pleasure of his will, To the praise of the glory of his grace, wherein he hath made us accepted in the beloved. In whom we have __(F) Redemption__ through his blood, the __(S) Forgiveness__ of sins, according to the riches of his grace; (Ephesians 1:5-7 KJV) [Reading: Ephesians 1]

6. And a stone of stumbling, and a rock of offence, even to them which stumble at the word, being disobedient: where unto also they were appointed. But ye are a _____(A) Chosen_____ generation, a royal priesthood, an holy nation, a peculiar people; that ye should shew forth the praises of him who hath called you out of darkness into his marvelous light; Which in time past were not a people, but are now the people of God: which had not obtained mercy, but now have obtained mercy. (1 Peter 2:8-10 KJV) [Reading: 1 Peter 2]

7. As every man hath received the gift, even so minister the same one to another, as good _____(P) Stewards_____ of the manifold grace of God. If any man speak, let him speak as the oracles of God; if any man minister, let him do it as of the ability which God giveth: that God in all things may be glorified __(M) Through__ Jesus Christ, to whom be praise and dominion for ever and ever. Amen. (1 Peter 4:10-11 KJV) [Reading: 1 Peter 4:1-12]

Chapter 4 Word-Search Puzzle Answers: Praise is what I do

Find the missing words from the passages in the word-search puzzle below.

Word List:

Chosen   Immediately   Firmament   Predestinated   Synagogue   Redemption

Instruments   Meek   Followed   Praise   Greatness   Darkness   Through

Receive   Cried   Stewards   Obscurity   Pharisees   Forgiveness

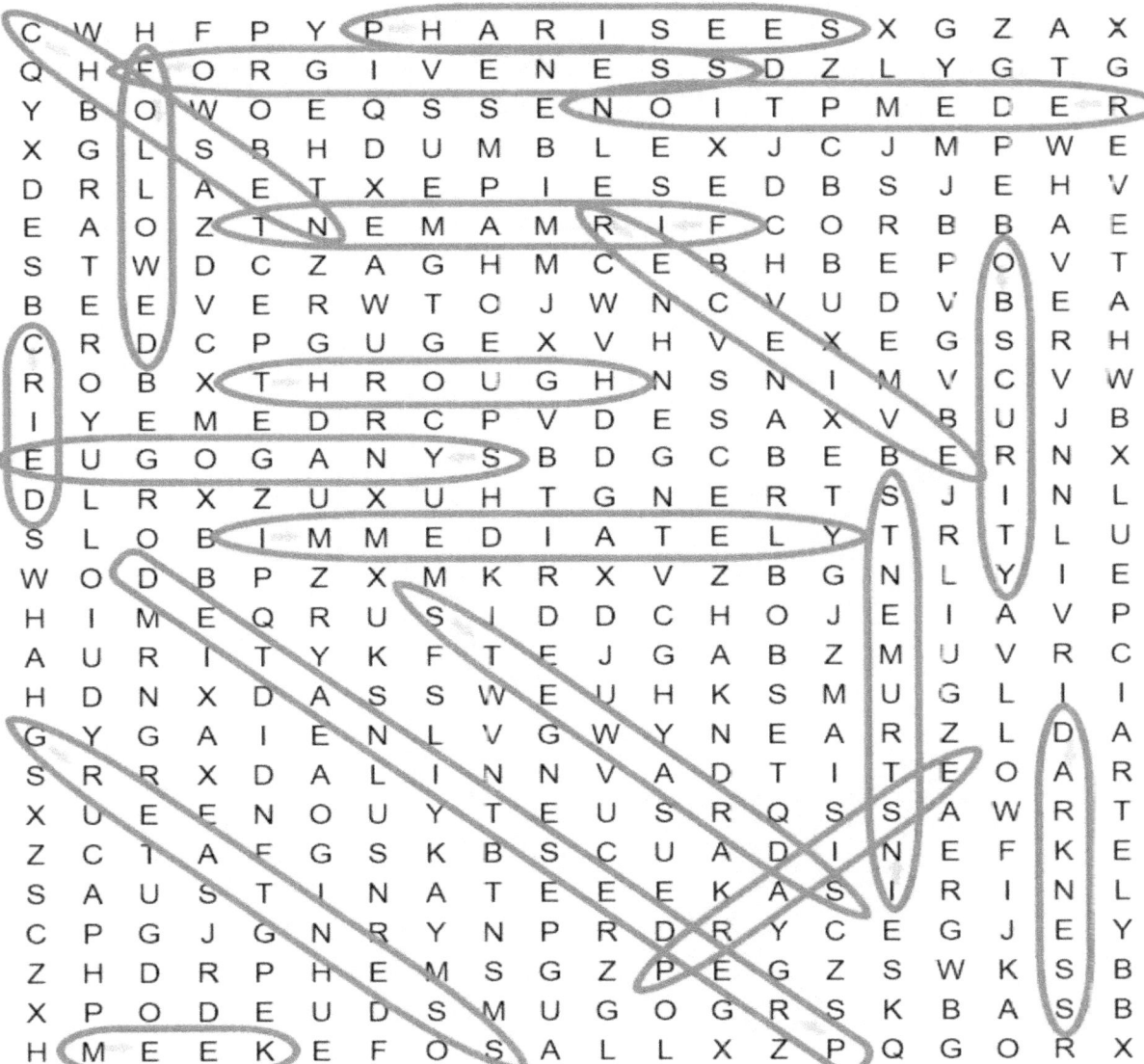

Puzzle 5 Answers: I believe in Jesus, I believe in God

Fill in the empty grid with the correct answers to the clues listed below. Each answer in the grid consist of one or more words. Use one letter per square.

Clues List:

Across

1 One of Jesus' disciples who walked on water.
4 What type of man did Jesus marvel at because of his great faith that he hasn't seen in all of Israel?
6 The 5th book of the Torah/Pentateuch/Law found in the holy bible.

Down

1 He is the author of the book of Romans.
2 Centurions were members of this group.
3 The mountain that the Lord gave to the children of Israel to take.
5 Who did it please when Jesus was bruised?

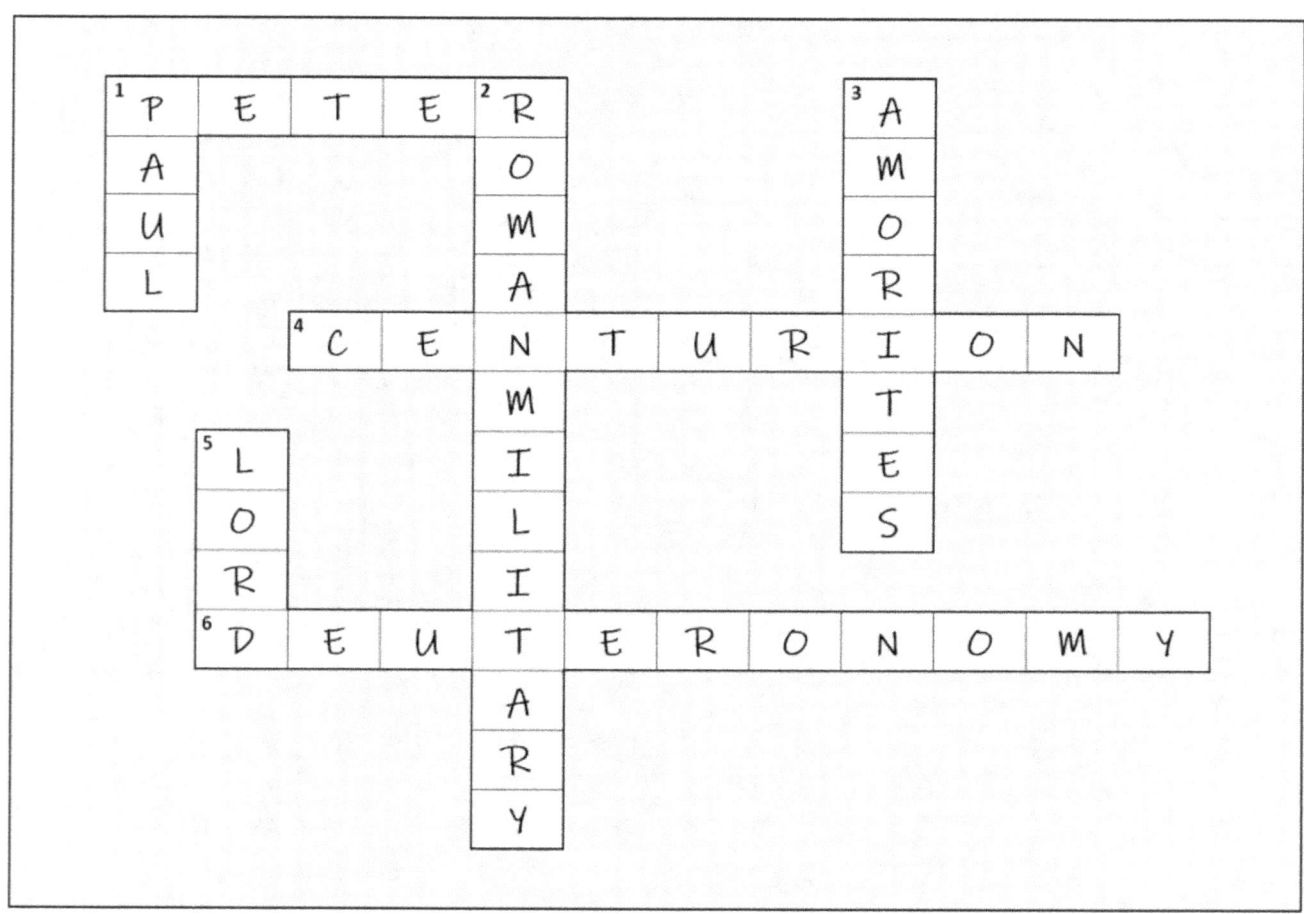

Puzzle 6 Answers: Not what I deserved, but what I deserve

Fill in the empty grid with the correct answers to the clues listed below. Each answer in the grid consist of one or more words. Use one letter per square.

Clues List:

Across

3 Who visited John to give him revelations on what is to come?

6 His Hebrew name means "God has Hidden" and the Author of the one of the books in the old testaments with less than 5 chapters.

7 Who confronted Peter in Antioch?

8 The Father gave Jesus, the good shepherd, the authority to lay down and take up his _____?

Down

1 What sea did Jesus walk by when he saw two brothers casting a net into the sea?

2 Ephesus, Smyrna, Pergamos, Thyatira, Sardis, Philadelphia, and Laodicea represents what in Asia?

4 Who was the Author of Psalms 103?

5 Who did Peter fear in Antioch that caused him to distance himself from the Gentiles?

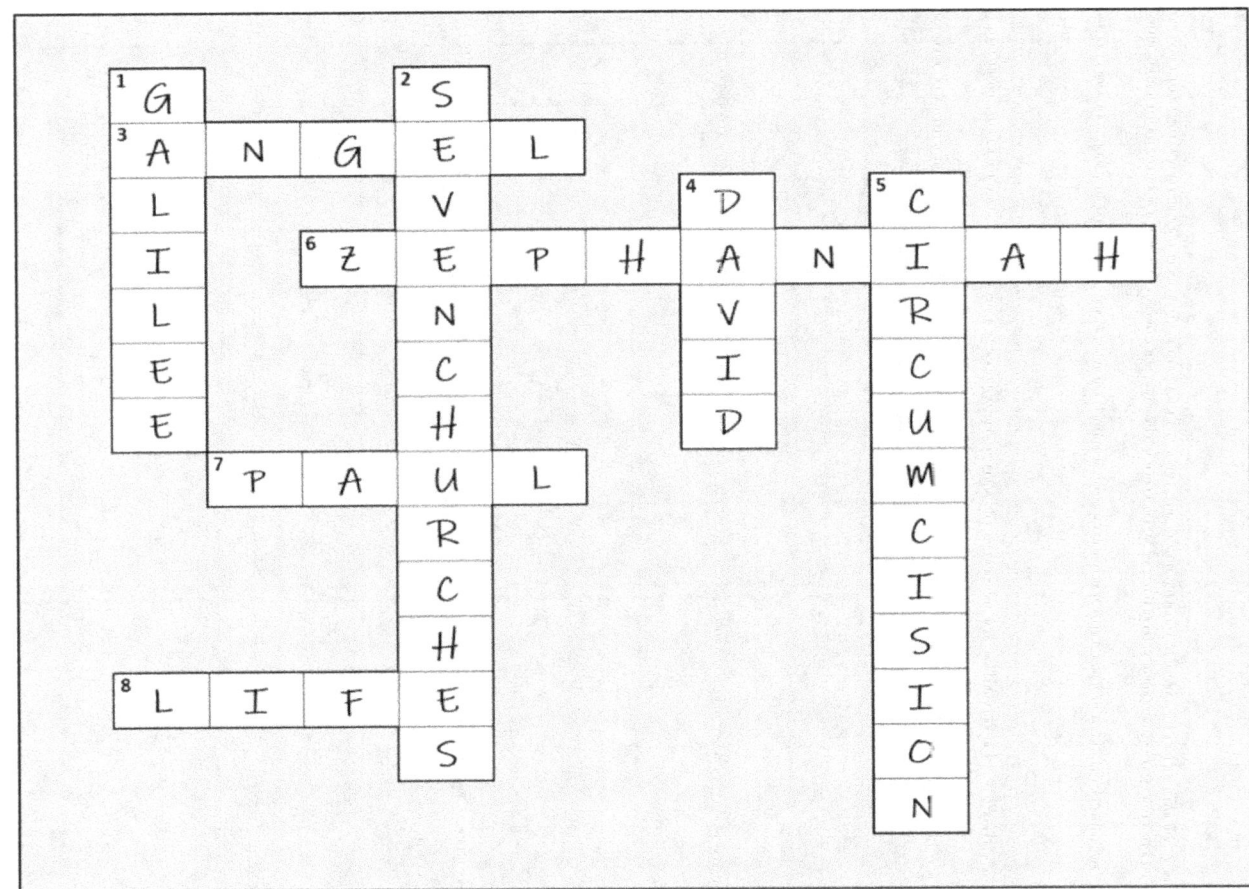

Puzzle 7 Answers: Be Encouraged

Fill in the empty grid with the correct answers to the clues listed below. Each answer in the grid consist of one or more words. Use one letter per square.

Clues List:

Across

1 The sins of _____ was written with iron on their hearts and their alters.
5 Paul's letters to the church at Corinth are found in this book.

Down

2 What does God search and test, even if it means giving the person according to their ways and actions?
3 Jesus was asked by his disciples to teach them how to pray because this person taught his disciples.
4 What book of the bible has the most chapters?

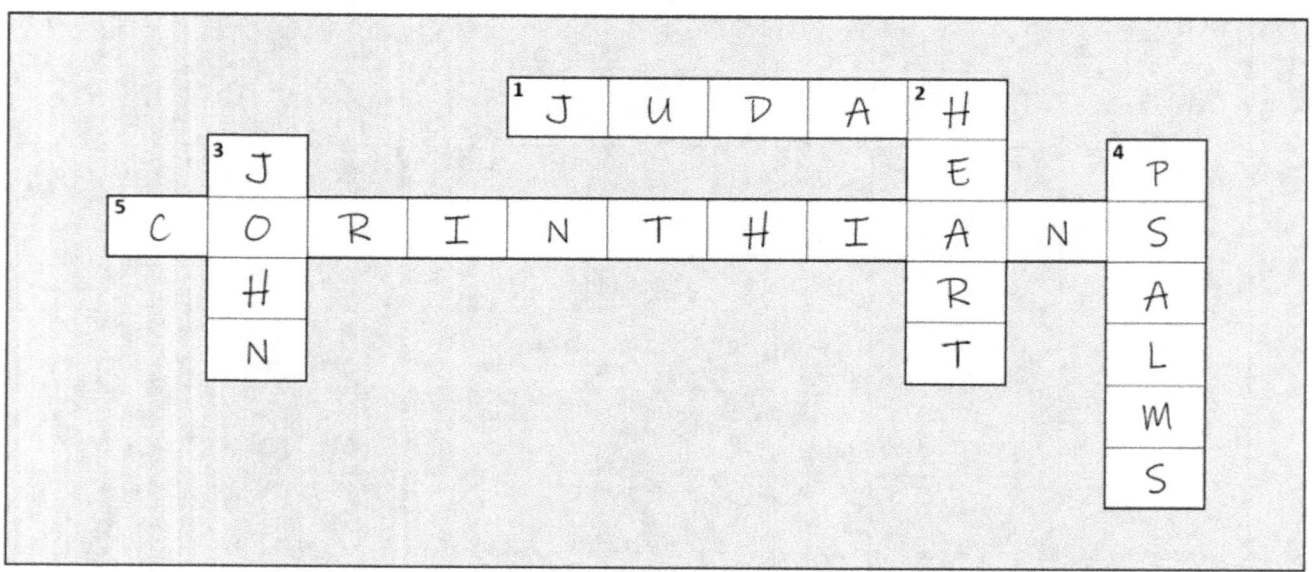

Puzzle 8 Answers: Praise is what I do

Fill in the empty grid with the correct answers to the clues listed below. Each answer in the grid consist of one or more words. Use one letter per square.

Clues List:

Across

2 Who was Jesus' and his disciples' treasurer?

4 What was the last name of Simon's son, that was a disciple and who would betray Jesus?

5 Jesus was a Galilean from this place.

6 Before the Passover, the Jews came to Bethany to see Jesus and this man.

Down

1 Jesus was also referred to as the son of this man.

2 The place where Jesus fulfilled the prophecy: "behold thy King cometh, sitting on an ass's colt."

3 Word that is often used to conclude a prayer or end of a letter.

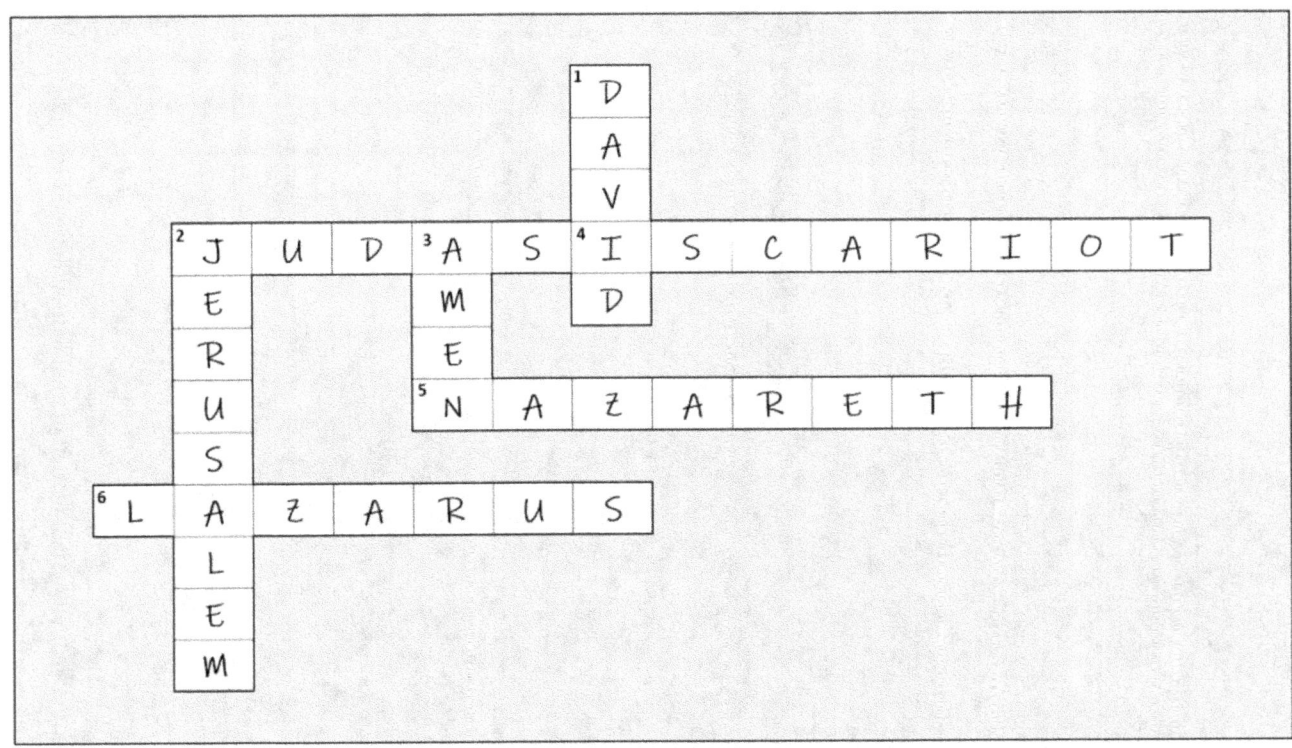

Index